ISBN 0-8373-5836-1
136 ADMISSION TEST SERIES

 *RUDMAN'S QUESTIONS AND ANSWERS ON THE...*

Certified Addictions Registered Nurse (CARN)

Intensive Preparation for the Examination

NATIONAL LEARNING CORPORATION

Copyright © 2018 by

National Learning Corporation

212 Michael Drive, Syosset, New York 11791

All rights reserved, including the right of reproduction in whole or in part, in any form or by any means, electronic or mechanical, including photocopying, recording, or by any information storage and retrieval system, without permission in writing from the Publisher.

(516) 921-8888
(800) 632-8888
(800) 645-6337
FAX: (516) 921-8743
www.passbooks.com
info @ passbooks.com

PRINTED IN THE UNITED STATES OF AMERICA

PASSBOOK®
NOTICE

This book is SOLELY intended for, is sold ONLY to, and its use is RESTRICTED to *individual*, bona fide applicants or candidates who qualify by virtue of having seriously filed applications for appropriate license, certificate, professional and/or promotional advancement, higher school matriculation, scholarship, or other legitimate requirements of educational and/or governmental authorities.

This book is NOT intended for use, class instruction, tutoring, training, duplication, copying, reprinting, excerption, or adaptation, etc., by:

(1) Other publishers

(2) Proprietors and/or Instructors of "Coaching" and/or Preparatory Courses

(3) Personnel and/or Training Divisions of commercial, industrial, and governmental organizations

(4) Schools, colleges, or universities and/or their departments and staffs, including teachers and other personnel

(5) Testing Agencies or Bureaus

(6) Study groups which seek by the purchase of a single volume to copy and/or duplicate and/or adapt this material for use by the group as a whole without having purchased individual volumes for each of the members of the group

(7) Et al.

Such persons would be in violation of appropriate Federal and State statutes.

PROVISION OF LICENSING AGREEMENTS. — Recognized educational commercial, industrial, and governmental institutions and organizations, and others legitimately engaged in educational pursuits, including training, testing, and measurement activities, may address a request for a licensing agreement to the copyright owners, who will determine whether, and under what conditions, including fees and charges, the materials in this book may be used by them. In other words, a licensing facility exists for the legitimate use of the material in this book on other than an individual basis. However, it is asseverated and affirmed here that the material in this book *CANNOT* be used without the receipt of the express permission of such a licensing agreement from the Publishers.

NATIONAL LEARNING CORPORATION
212 Michael Drive
Syosset, New York 11791

Inquiries re licensing agreements should be addressed to:
The President
National Learning Corporation
212 Michael Drive
Syosset, New York 11791

PASSBOOK® SERIES

THE *PASSBOOK® SERIES* has been created to prepare applicants and candidates for the ultimate academic battlefield – the examination room.

At some time in our lives, each and every one of us may be required to take an examination – for validation, matriculation, admission, qualification, registration, certification, or licensure.

Based on the assumption that every applicant or candidate has met the basic formal educational standards, has taken the required number of courses, and read the necessary texts, the *PASSBOOK® SERIES* furnishes the one special preparation which may assure passing with confidence, instead of failing with insecurity. Examination questions – together with answers – are furnished as the basic vehicle for study so that the mysteries of the examination and its compounding difficulties may be eliminated or diminished by a sure method.

This book is meant to help you pass your examination provided that you qualify and are serious in your objective.

The entire field is reviewed through the huge store of content information which is succinctly presented through a provocative and challenging approach – the question-and-answer method.

A climate of success is established by furnishing the correct answers at the end of each test.

You soon learn to recognize types of questions, forms of questions, and patterns of questioning. You may even begin to anticipate expected outcomes.

You perceive that many questions are repeated or adapted so that you can gain acute insights, which may enable you to score many sure points.

You learn how to confront new questions, or types of questions, and to attack them confidently and work out the correct answers.

You note objectives and emphases, and recognize pitfalls and dangers, so that you may make positive educational adjustments.

Moreover, you are kept fully informed in relation to new concepts, methods, practices, and directions in the field.

You discover that you are actually taking the examination all the time: you are preparing for the examination by "taking" an examination, not by reading extraneous and/or supererogatory textbooks.

In short, this PASSBOOK®, used directedly, should be an important factor in helping you to pass your test.

CERTIFIED ADDICTIONS
REGISTERED NURSE (CARN) EXAMINATION

INTRODUCTION

Administered by the Addictions Nursing Certification Board (ANCB), the Certified Addictions Registered Nurse (CARN) examination is a 200-question test designed to assess specialized knowledge of addictions nursing practice. The exam is four hours long and consists entirely of multiple-choice questions.

The CARN examination determines the nurse's ability to apply knowledge from nursing and related disciplines in the care of persons with problems relating to patterns of abuse, dependence and addictions, as well as the ability to synthesize the nursing process in the care of persons with potential or actual problems with such patterns.

Most of the questions on the CARN exam focus on concurrent diagnosis (including concurrent physical and addiction diagnoses, concurrent psychiatric and addiction diagnoses, and polysubstance abuse). Other content areas covered on the exam are depressant substances, stimulant substances, process addictions, and hallucinogenic substances. Relating to nursing diagnoses and general practice, the test questions are broken down almost equally between five areas – cognitive, psychosocial, spiritual and biological needs, as well as general scope of practice.

To be eligible to take the certification exam, candidates must hold a current, full and unrestricted license as a registered nurse in the United States, its possessions or Canada; have three years of experience as a practicing registered nurse; and have a minimum of 4,000 hours of nursing experience related to addictions as a registered nurse in a staff, administrative, teaching, private practice, consultation, counseling or research capacity within the five years prior to application. For additional eligibility information, consult the CARN exam information on the International Nurses Society on Addictions website – www.intnsa.org – or other nursing information resources.

Candidates will be notified of their test scores approximately six weeks after test administration. Those who pass the certification exam will be notified within one week, and those who fail will receive a detailed breakdown of their scaled score and in which areas their performance was at its strongest and weakest. Candidates can retake the CARN examination as often as they wish.

Table 1. Blueprint for CARN and CARN,AP related to client problems

Area	%
Concurrent diagnosis (includes concurrent physical and addiction diagnoses, concurrent psychiatric and addiction diagnoses, and polysubstance abuse)	35
Depressant substances	25
Stimulant substances	20
Process addictions (includes eating disorders, gambling, spending, sexual addictions)	15
Hallucinogenic substances	5

Table 2. Blueprint for CARN & CARN,AP related to nursing diagnosis and general practice

Area	%
Cognitive needs	21
Psychosocial needs	20
Spiritual needs	20
Biological needs	19
General scope of practice	20

1. For one week, Mr. Simon Lane has been a patient on the detoxification unit for alcoholism and occasional use of marijuana and cocaine. He is now in small group therapy sessions led by a nurse. On his second meeting, he fidgets in his seat and finally says, "I'm having difficulty sitting still. Am I bothering some of you who are here? Maybe I should stop coming to these meetings." Which of these actions in response to Mr. Lane would be appropriate?

   1. Encourage him to share his problem with the group members and ask for their help.

   1. Recognize that this is manipulative behavior and encourage him to remain in the group.

   2. Remove him from the group and further assess his needs.

   3. Tell him not to concern himself about the group members and to continue in the group.

Key 1

3. Mrs. Lora Green, 50 year old, is admitted to the detoxification unit for heavy drinking. Her breathalyzer blood alcohol level is 0.10%. Her orders include oxazepam (Serax) 10 mg q 3-4h prn and diphenhydramine hydrochloride (Benadryl) 50 mg q 6h prn. During the nurse's initial assessment of Mrs. Green, which of thee questions should take priority?

   1. Has she been taking any over-the-counter medication?

   2. Has she ever had a withdrawal seizure?

   3. When did she have her last drink?

   4. What has been her usual daily alcohol consumption?

Key 3

2. Mr. Bruce Mann, who is on the chemical dependency unit, tells the nurse that he is having cravings for cocaine. In addition to acknowledging the discomfort, the nurse suggests that he exercise at the gym, where various exercise machines are available. The appropriateness of this decision is based on which of these understandings about cocaine addicts?

   1. They are more comfortable alone.

   2. They need to be kept mentally occupied.

   3. They are highly motivated to improve their physique.

   4. They need outlets for physical tension to reduce craving.

Key 4

4. Mr. Larry Port, 31 years old, who is on the addictions unit, last used cannabis (marijuana) 48 hours ago. A drug screen was administered to him. The results will most likely be positive for marijuana. A positive result will remain for

   1. several weeks.

   2. seven days.

   3. 48 hours.

   4. an undetermined period.

Key 1

DESCRIPTION OF THE CARN,AP EXAMINATION

The CARN,AP examination was developed following a practice (job) analysis of addictions nursing completed by IntNSA in 1996. Nearly 40% of the 450 survey respondents reported holding a master's or higher degree. Data analysis revealed significant differences between the practice patterns of nurses with graduate preparation and nurses with less preparation.

Although both groups of nurses dealt with similar clients, the master's-prepared nurses placed greater emphasis on psychotherapeutic interventions for clients, as well as a broader view of the client as a member of a family, group, and community. After reviewing the findings, the ANCB developed a blueprint for the advanced practice examination.

Like the CARN exam, the CARN,AP exam addresses biological, psychosocial, cognitive, and spiritual problems resulting from concurrent diagnoses (multiple diagnoses); depressant, stimulant, and hallucinogenic substances; and process addictions (e.g., eating disorders, gambling, sexual addiction, co-dependency). The percentage of test content assigned to client problems, nursing diagnoses and general practice is the same as the CARN exam noted in the section above. However, the content of the advanced practice exam differs from the generalist CARN exam in having greater emphasis in the following areas:

- Counseling clients and families.
- Clients within the family system.
- Case finding; Continuum of care.
- Integration of theory.
- Group dynamics; Therapeutic role of the nurse in groups.
- Education of families and public about addictions.
- Cultural needs of client and family.
- Teaching problem solving to client and family.
- Primary prevention activities.
- Psychobiology (neurotransmitters, endorphins, etc.).
- Application of research in practice.
- Quality/performance improvement;
- Outcomes measures; Benchmarking.
- Legal/ethical issues.

The CARN,AP exam consists of 200 multiple-choice items, many written in case situations. It is four hours in length.

HOW TO TAKE A TEST

You have studied long, hard and conscientiously.

With your official admission card in hand, and your heart pounding, you have been admitted to the examination room.

You note that there are several hundred other applicants in the examination room waiting to take the same test.

They all appear to be equally well prepared.

You know that nothing but your best effort will suffice. The "moment of truth" is at hand: you now have to demonstrate objectively, in writing, your knowledge of content and your understanding of subject matter.

You are fighting the most important battle of your life—to pass and/or score high on an examination which will determine your career and provide the economic basis for your livelihood.

What extra, special things should you know and should you do in taking the examination?

I. YOU MUST PASS AN EXAMINATION

A. *WHAT EVERY CANDIDATE SHOULD KNOW*

Examination applicants often ask us for help in preparing for the written test. What can I study in advance? What kinds of questions will be asked? How will the test be given? How will the papers be graded?

B. *HOW ARE EXAMS DEVELOPED?*

Examinations are carefully written by trained technicians who are specialists in the field known as "psychological measurement," in consultation with recognized authorities in the field of work that the test will cover. These experts recommend the subject matter areas or skills to be tested; only those knowledges or skills important to your success on the job are included. The most reliable books and source materials available are used as references. Together, the experts and technicians judge the difficulty level of the questions.

Test technicians know how to phrase questions so that the problem is clearly stated. Their ethics do not permit "trick" or "catch" questions. Questions may have been tried out on sample groups, or subjected to statistical analysis, to determine their usefulness.

Written tests are often used in combination with performance tests, ratings of training and experience, and oral interviews. All of these measures combine to form the best-known means of finding the right person for the right job.

II. HOW TO PASS THE WRITTEN TEST

A. BASIC STEPS

1) Study the announcement

How, then, can you know what subjects to study? Our best answer is: "Learn as much as possible about the class of positions for which you've applied." The exam will test the knowledge, skills and abilities needed to do the work.

Your most valuable source of information about the position you want is the official exam announcement. This announcement lists the training and experience qualifications. Check these standards and apply only if you come reasonably close to meeting them. Many jurisdictions preview the written test in the exam announcement by including a section called "Knowledge and Abilities Required," "Scope of the Examination," or some similar heading. Here you will find out specifically what fields will be tested.

2) Choose appropriate study materials

If the position for which you are applying is technical or advanced, you will read more advanced, specialized material. If you are already familiar with the basic principles of your field, elementary textbooks would waste your time. Concentrate on advanced textbooks and technical periodicals. Think through the concepts and review difficult problems in your field.

These are all general sources. You can get more ideas on your own initiative, following these leads. For example, training manuals and publications of the government agency which employs workers in your field can be useful, particularly for technical and professional positions. A letter or visit to the government department involved may result in more specific study suggestions, and certainly will provide you with a more definite idea of the exact nature of the position you are seeking.

3) Study this book!

III. KINDS OF TESTS

Tests are used for purposes other than measuring knowledge and ability to perform specified duties. For some positions, it is equally important to test ability to make adjustments to new situations or to profit from training. In others, basic mental abilities not dependent on information are essential. Questions which test these things may not appear as pertinent to the duties of the position as those which test for knowledge and information. Yet they are often highly important parts of a fair examination. For very general questions, it is almost impossible to help you direct your study efforts. What we can do is to point out some of the more common of these general abilities needed in public service positions and describe some typical questions.

1) General information

Broad, general information has been found useful for predicting job success in some kinds of work. This is tested in a variety of ways, from vocabulary lists to questions about current events. Basic background in some field of work, such as sociology or economics, may be sampled in a group of questions. Often these are principles which have become familiar to most persons through exposure rather than through formal training. It is difficult to advise you how to study for these questions; being alert to the world around you is our best suggestion.

2) Verbal ability

An example of an ability needed in many positions is verbal or language ability. Verbal ability is, in brief, the ability to use and understand words. Vocabulary and grammar tests are typical measures of this ability. Reading comprehension or paragraph interpretation questions are common in many kinds of civil service tests. You are given a paragraph of written material and asked to find its central meaning.

IV. KINDS OF QUESTIONS

1. Multiple-choice Questions

Most popular of the short-answer questions is the "multiple choice" or "best answer" question. It can be used, for example, to test for factual knowledge, ability to solve problems or judgment in meeting situations found at work.

A multiple-choice question is normally one of three types—ending. You are to find

- It can begin with an incomplete statement followed by several possible one ending which best completes the statement, although some of the others may not be entirely wrong.
- It can also be a complete statement in the form of a question which is answered by choosing one of the statements listed.
- It can be in the form of a problem — again you select the best answer.

Here is an example of a multiple-choice question with a discussion which should give you some clues as to the method for choosing the right answer:

When an employee has a complaint about his assignment, the action which will *best* help him overcome his difficulty is to
- A. discuss his difficulty with his coworkers
- B. take the problem to the head of the organization
- C. take the problem to the person who gave him the assignment
- D. say nothing to anyone about his complaint

In answering this question, you should study each of the choices to find which is best. Consider choice "A" — Certainly an employee may discuss his complaint with fellow employees, but no change or improvement can result, and the complaint remains unresolved. Choice "B" is a poor choice since the head of the organization probably does not know what assignment you have been given, and taking your problem to him is known as "going over the head" of the supervisor. The supervisor, or person who made the assignment, is the person who can clarify it or correct any injustice. Choice "C" is, therefore, correct. To say nothing, as in choice "D," is unwise. Supervisors have and interest in knowing the problems employees are facing, and the employee is seeking a solution to his problem. More difficult is the combination multiple-choice question which involves picking several correct or wrong choices from the four or five given.

2. True/False

3. Matching Questions

Matching an answer from a column of choices with another column.

V. RECORDING YOUR ANSWERS

Computer terminals are used more and more today for many different kinds of exams.

For an examination with very few applicants, you may be told to record your answers in the test booklet itself. Separate answer sheets are much more common. If this separate answer sheet is to be scored by machine — and this is often the case — it is highly important that you mark your answers correctly in order to get credit.

VI. BEFORE THE TEST

YOUR PHYSICAL CONDITION IS IMPORTANT

If you are not well, you can't do your best work on tests. If you are half asleep, you can't do your best either. Here are some tips:

1) Get about the same amount of sleep you usually get. Don't stay up all night before the test, either partying or worrying—DON'T DO IT!
2) If you wear glasses, be sure to wear them when you go to take the test. This goes for hearing aids, too.
3) If you have any physical problems that may keep you from doing your best, be sure to tell the person giving the test. If you are sick or in poor health, you really cannot do your best on any test. You can always come back and take the test some other time.

Common sense will help you find procedures to follow to get ready for an examination. Too many of us, however, overlook these sensible measures. Indeed, nervousness and fatigue have been found to be the most serious reasons why applicants fail to do their best on civil service tests. Here is a list of reminders:

- Begin your preparation early — Don't wait until the last minute to go scurrying around for books and materials or to find out what the position is all about.
- Prepare continuously — An hour a night for a week is better than an all-night cram session. This has been definitely established. What is more, a night a week for a month will return better dividends than crowding your study into a shorter period of time.
- Locate the place of the exam — You have been sent a notice telling you when and where to report for the examination. If the location is in a different town or otherwise unfamiliar to you, it would be well to inquire the best route and learn something about the building.
- Relax the night before the test — Allow your mind to rest. Do not study at all that night. Plan some mild recreation or diversion; then go to bed early and get a good night's sleep.
- Get up early enough to make a leisurely trip to the place for the test — This way unforeseen events, traffic snarls, unfamiliar buildings, etc. will not upset you.
- Dress comfortably — A written test is not a fashion show. You will be known by number and not by name, so wear something comfortable.
- Leave excess paraphernalia at home — Shopping bags and odd bundles will get in your way. You need bring only the items mentioned in the official notice you received; usually everything you need is provided. Do not bring reference books to the exam. They will only confuse those last minutes and be taken away from you when in the test room.

- Arrive somewhat ahead of time — If because of transportation schedules you must get there very early, bring a newspaper or magazine to take your mind off yourself while waiting.
- Locate the examination room — When you have found the proper room, you will be directed to the seat or part of the room where you will sit. Sometimes you are given a sheet of instructions to read while you are waiting. Do not fill out any forms until you are told to do so; just read them and be prepared.
- Relax and prepare to listen to the instructions
- If you have any physical problem that may keep you from doing your best, be sure to tell the test administrator. If you are sick or in poor health, you really cannot do your best on the exam. You can come back and take the test some other time.

VII. AT THE TEST

The day of the test is here and you have the test booklet in your hand. The temptation to get going is very strong. Caution! There is more to success than knowing the right answers. You must know how to identify your papers and understand variations in the type of short-answer question used in this particular examination. Follow these suggestions for maximum results from your efforts:

1) Cooperate with the monitor
The test administrator has a duty to create a situation in which you can be as much at ease as possible. He will give instructions, tell you when to begin, check to see that you are marking your answer sheet correctly, and so on. He is not there to guard you, although he will see that your competitors do not take unfair advantage. He wants to help you do your best.

2) Listen to all instructions
Don't jump the gun! Wait until you understand all directions. In most civil service tests you get more time than you need to answer the questions. So don't be in a hurry. Read each word of instructions until you clearly understand the meaning. Study the examples, listen to all announcements and follow directions. Ask questions if you do not understand what to do.

3) Identify your papers
Exams are usually identified by number only. You will be assigned a number; you must not put your name on your test papers. Be sure to copy your number correctly. Since more than one exam may be given, copy your exact examination title.

4) Plan your time
Unless you are told that a test is a "speed" or "rate of work" test, speed itself is usually not important. Time enough to answer all the questions will be provided, but this does not mean that you have all day. An overall time limit has been set. Divide the total time (in minutes) by the number of questions to determine the approximate time you have for each question.

5) Do not linger over difficult questions
If you come across a difficult question, mark it with a paper clip (useful to have along) and come back to it when you have been through the booklet. One caution if you do this — be sure to skip a number on your answer sheet as well. Check often to be sure that

you have not lost your place and that you are marking in the row numbered the same as the question you are answering.

6) Read the questions

Be sure you know what the question asks! Many capable people are unsuccessful because they failed to *read* the questions correctly.

7) Answer all questions

Unless you have been instructed that a penalty will be deducted for incorrect answers, it is better to guess than to omit a question.

8) Speed tests

It is often better NOT to guess on speed tests. It has been found that on timed tests people are tempted to spend the last few seconds before time is called in marking answers at random — without even reading them — in the hope of picking up a few extra points. To discourage this practice, the instructions may warn you that your score will be "corrected" for guessing. That is, a penalty will be applied. The incorrect answers will be deducted from the correct ones, or some other penalty formula will be used.

9) Review your answers

If you finish before time is called, go back to the questions you guessed or omitted to give them further thought. Review other answers if you have time.

10) Return your test materials

If you are ready to leave before others have finished or time is called, take ALL your materials to the monitor and leave quietly. Never take any test material with you. The monitor can discover whose papers are not complete, and taking a test booklet may be grounds for disqualification.

VIII. EXAMINATION TECHNIQUES

1) Read the general instructions carefully. These are usually printed on the first page of the exam booklet. As a rule, these instructions refer to the timing of the examination; the fact that you should not start work until the signal and must stop work at a signal, etc. If there are any *special* instructions, such as a choice of questions to be answered, make sure that you note this instruction carefully.

2) When you are ready to start work on the examination, that is as soon as the signal has been given, read the instructions to each question booklet, underline any key words or phrases, such as *least, best, outline, describe* and the like. In this way you will tend to answer as requested rather than discover on reviewing your paper that you *listed without describing,* that you selected the *worst* choice rather than the *best* choice, etc.

3) If the examination is of the objective or multiple-choice type — that is, each question will also give a series of possible answers: A, B, C or D, and you are called upon to select the best answer and write the letter next to that answer on your answer paper — it is advisable to start answering each question in turn. There may be anywhere from 50 to 100 such questions in the three or four hours allotted and you can see how much time would be taken if you read through all the questions before beginning to answer any.

Furthermore, if you come across a question or group of questions which you know would be difficult to answer, it would undoubtedly affect your handling of all the other questions.

4) If the examination is of the essay type and contains but a few questions, it is a moot point as to whether you should read all the questions before starting to answer any one. Of course, if you are given a choice — say five out of seven and the like — then it is essential to read all the questions so you can eliminate the two that are most difficult. If, however, you are asked to answer all the questions, there may be danger in trying to answer the easiest one first because you may find that you will spend too much time on it. The best technique is to answer the first question, then proceed to the second, etc.

5) Time your answers. Before the exam begins, write down the time it started, then add the time allowed for the examination and write down the time it must be completed, then divide the time available somewhat as follows:
   - If 3-1/2 hours are allowed, that would be 210 minutes. If you have 80 objective-type questions, that would be an average of 2-1/2 minutes per question. Allow yourself no more than 2 minutes per question, or a total of 160 minutes, which will permit about 50 minutes to review.

   - If for the time allotment of 210 minutes there are 7 essay questions to answer, that would average about 30 minutes a question. Give yourself only 25 minutes per question so that you have about 35 minutes to review.

6) The most important instruction is to *read each question* and make sure you know what is wanted. The second most important instruction is to *time yourself properly* so that you answer every question. The third most important instruction is to *answer every question*. Guess if you have to but include something for each question. Remember that you will receive no credit for a blank and will probably receive some credit if you write something in answer to an essay question. If you guess a letter — say "B" for a multiple-choice question — you may have guessed right. If you leave a blank as an answer to a multiple-choice question, the examiners may respect your feelings but it will not add a point to your score. Some exams may penalize you for wrong answers, so in such cases *only,* you may not want to guess unless you have some basis for your answer.

7) Suggestions
   a. Objective-type questions
      1. Examine the question booklet for proper sequence of pages and questions
      2. Read all instructions carefully
      3. Skip any question which seems too difficult; return to it after all other questions have been answered
      4. Apportion your time properly; do not spend too much time on any single question or group of questions
      5. Note and underline key words — *all, most, fewest, least, best, worst, same, opposite,* etc.
      6. Pay particular attention to negatives
      7. Note unusual option, e.g., unduly long, short, complex, different or similar in content to the body of the question
      8. Observe the use of "hedging" words — *probably, may, most likely,* etc.
      9. Make sure that your answer is put next to the same number as the question

10. Do not second-guess unless you have good reason to believe the second answer is definitely more correct
11. Cross out original answer if you decide another answer is more accurate; do not erase until you are ready to hand your paper in
12. Answer all questions; guess unless instructed otherwise
13. Leave time for review

    b. Essay questions
        1 Read each question carefully
        2. Determine exactly what is wanted. Underline key words or phrases.
        3. Decide on outline or paragraph answer
        4. Include many different points and elements unless asked to develop any one or two points or elements
        5. Show impartiality by giving pros and cons unless directed to select one side only
        6. Make and write down any assumptions you find necessary to answer the questions
        7. Watch your English, grammar, punctuation and choice of words
        8. Time your answers; don't crowd material

8) Answering the essay question

Most essay questions can be answered by framing the specific response around several key words or ideas. Here are a few such key words or ideas:

M's: manpower, materials, methods, money, management
P's: purpose, program, policy, plan, procedure, practice, problems,
    pitfalls, personnel, public relations
    a. Six basic steps in handling problems:
        1. Preliminary plan and background development
        2. Collect information, data and facts
        3. Analyze and interpret information, data and facts
        4. Analyze and develop solutions as well as make recommendations
        5. Prepare report and sell recommendations
        6. Install recommendations and follow up effectiveness

    b. Pitfalls to avoid
        1. *Taking things for granted* — A statement of the situation does not necessarily imply that each of the elements is necessarily true; for example, a complaint may be invalid and biased so that all that can be taken for granted is that a complaint has been registered
        2. *Considering only one side of a situation* — Wherever possible, indicate several alternatives and then point out the reasons you selected the best one
        3. *Failing to indicate follow up* — Whenever your answer indicates action on your part, make certain that you will take proper follow-up action to see how successful your recommendations, procedures or actions turn out to be
        4. *Taking too long in answering any single question* — Remember to time your answers properly

EXAMINATION SECTION

EXAMINATION SECTION
TEST 1

DIRECTIONS: Each question or incomplete statement is followed by several suggested answers or completions. Select the one that BEST answers the question or completes the statement. *PRINT THE LETTER OF THE CORRECT ANSWER IN THE SPACE AT THE RIGHT.*

1. Which of the following is NOT a genetically influenced risk/protective factor for alcohol dependence?
    A. The alcohol metabolizing enzyme aldehyde dehydrogenase
    B. High levels of impulsivity/sensations seeking/disinhibition
    C. Low levels of impulsivity/sensations seeking/disinhibition
    D. Low level of response to alcohol

    1.____

2. Large epidemiological studies have shown that heart disease risk reduction with moderate alcohol consumption is generally between
    A. 30% and 45%   B. 5% and 10%
    C. 10% and 15%   D. 50% and 75%

    2.____

3. What percentage of people who drink have experienced an alcohol-related problem?
    A. 10%   B. 20%   C. 30%   D. 40%

    3.____

4. A standard drink is generally defined as _____ ounce(s) of 80-proof distilled spirits, _____ ounces of wine, and _____ ounces of beer.
    A. 1; 4; 8   B. 1.5; 4; 8   C. 1; 4; 12   D. 1.5; 5; 12

    4.____

5. Moderate drinking is defined as
    A. no more than two drinks a day for women
    B. no more than three drinks a day for men
    C. one drink a day for men and women
    D. no more than one drink a day for women and two drinks a day for men

    5.____

6. All of the following are true, EXCEPT:
    A. Moderate alcohol intake reduces all-cause mortality primarily due to its ability to decrease cardiovascular diseases, most especially coronary heart disease.
    B. Those who abstain from alcohol have a decreased incidence of cardiovascular disease when compared to moderate consumers.
    C. Light to moderate alcohol intake from beer, wine or spirits is associated with a reduction in all-cause mortality.
    D. The relationship between alcohol intake and reduced risk of coronary disease is generally accepted as a U-shaped curve of low-dose protective effect and higher doses producing a loss of protective effects and increased all-cause deaths.

    6.____

7. All of the following are true about alcohol dependence and depression, EXCEPT: 7.____
    A. As many as 80% of alcoholic men and women complain of depressive symptoms, an at least a third meet the criteria for major depressive disorder.
    B. Treatment professionals have found that after two or three weeks of abstinence from alcohol, and with good nutrition, the temporary depressive effects of alcohol dissipate.
    C. Both have the same etiology.
    D. Approximately 85% of individuals who commit suicide suffer from depression or alcohol dependence.

8. All of the following conditions increase the risk of developing an alcohol use disorder, EXCEPT   8.____
    A. bipolar disorder
    B. schizophrenia
    C. ADHD without conduct problems
    D. antisocial personality disorder

9. Excessive chronic alcohol use is associated with all of the following, EXCEPT   9.____
    A. impaired body utilization of vitamins
    B. low resistance to bacterial infections
    C. weight gain
    D. sleep disorders

10. Among chronic heavy drinkers, the MOST common pre-existing condition in the liver prior to cirrhosis is   10.____
    A. viral hepatitis
    B. fatty liver
    C. cholelithiasis
    D. thrombosis of the portal vein

11. Which of the following is NOT true about alcohol withdrawal symptoms?   11.____
    A. Symptoms include sweating, rapid heartbeat, hypertension, tremors, anorexia, insomnia, agitation, anxiety, nausea, and vomiting.
    B. 15% of alcoholics progress from the autonomic hyperactivity and agitation common to withdrawal from other drugs to seizures and, for some, even death.
    C. Pharmacological management of acute alcohol withdrawal generally involves the use of benzodiazepines.
    D. Once these symptoms are treated, relapse is unlikely.

12. Clues to alcohol abuse and dependence may include all of the following, EXCEPT   12.____
    A. elevated values for SGOT, LDH, cholesterol, GGT, MCV and other tests
    B. broken bones
    C. elevated mood and increased energy
    D. anxiety or panic attacks

13. Which of the following is NOT one of the diagnostic criteria for alcohol abuse?   13.____
    A. Tolerance
    B. Repeated alcohol consumption when it could be physically dangerous
    C. Repeated alcohol-related legal problems such as arrests
    D. Continued drinking despite interpersonal or social problems that are caused or made worse by drinking

14. Alcohol affects numerous neurotransmitters in the brain. The systems   14.____
    affected that may have a genetic influence on alcohol dependence include:
    A. The dopamine system   B. The serotonin system
    C. The GABA system   D. All of the above

15. Certain questions are useful in screening to determine presence of ethanol   15.____
    dependence. One such set of questions is known as the "CAGE"
    questionnaire. This is an acronym, which stands for
    A. Chloral hydrate (noctec), Alcohol, Glutethimide (doriden), Ethclorvynol (Placidyl)
    B. Cut down, Annoyed, Guilty, Eye-opener
    C. Confusion, Agitation, S3 Gallop, Edema
    D. un-Controllable urge to drink, un-Able to limit intake, un-Grateful for help to stop drinking, un-Excited about treatment

16. All of the following are common elements of brief intervention, EXCEPT   16.____
    A. confrontational counseling style   B. feedback of personal risk
    C. advice to change   D. responsibility of the patient

17. All of these statements about Alcoholics Anonymous are generally true,   17.____
    EXCEPT:
    A. There are no dues.
    B. Anyone can become a member.
    C. Belief in God is a pre-requisite to join.
    D. Research has shown this approach to be effective.

18. Cognitive-behavioral therapies (CBTs)   18.____
    A. are based on social learning and behavioral theories of drug abuse
    B. can be summarized as "recognize, avoid, and cope"
    C. are focused on strategies for coping with craving, fostering motivation to change, managing thoughts about drugs, developing problem-solving skills, planning for and managing high-risk situations, and cultivating drug refusal skills
    D. all of the above

Questions 19-21.

DIRECTIONS: Questions 19 through 21 are based on the following passage.

Leslie is 19 years of age and weighs 115 pounds. She is a college freshman living away from home for the first time. She visits the Student Health Center on campus for concern about possible sexually transmitted disease (STD) exposure. When asked if she had unprotected sex, she says she doesn't remember. She says that over the weekend she went to an off-campus party. The party started at 7:00 and she remembers consuming six 12 oz. cans of beer and two 1.5 oz. shots of 80-proof distilled spirits during the first 4 hours of the party. She does not remember how the party ended, how she got back to her dorm room or what happened before she got there. She is concerned that her drinking may be a problem.

19. What screening tool could you use to determine if Leslie has a drinking   19.____
    problem?
    A. The CAPA or ADICT
    B. The CAGE or AUDIT
    C. The Ham-D or MAST
    D. None of the above; it is obvious that she is alcohol dependent

20. How much alcohol did Leslie consume during the first four hours of the party?   20.____
    A. The equivalent of 8 standard drinks
    B. About 75 ounces
    C. More than what would be considered a "binge"
    D. All of the above

21. Does Leslie appear to be a candidate for brief intervention?   21.____
    A. No, what she really needs is inpatient treatment.
    B. Yes, because studies have shown the effectiveness of brief intervention
       for alcohol abuse, and having already had an adverse consequence, she
       may be more likely to consider changing her behavior.
    C. If this was the only time that she had an alcohol-related problem, she
       would not need intervention.
    D. Yes, because pharmacotherapy and counseling could prevent future
       binge drinking.

Questions 22-24.

DIRECTIONS: Questions 22 through 24 are based on the following passage.

Steve is a male 55 years of age who until recently was a mid-level manager at a local bank. He presents to his family physician with complaints of sleep problems, feeling down for the past three weeks, loss of interest in activities, loss of interest in sex, decreased appetite and weight loss. Because he is depressed, he is screened for depression and suicide risk. He denies any thoughts or plans of suicide. When asked about alcohol consumption, he admits to having 2 or 3 drinks per day. When asked about the type of alcohol consumed and the amount per drink, he states that he usually mixes 3 ounces of vodka with 5 ounces of orange juice for each drink. He also describes experiencing problems getting along with his family. He is screened with the CAGE questions and responds positive for all four items. He states that when he tries to stop drinking he gets the "shakes." The family physician thinks Steve may be alcohol dependent and depressed and that he may need a psychiatric or addiction medicine referral.

22. Is Steve's alcohol consumption close to what is described moderate drinking?   22.____
    A. Yes, he drinks 2 to 3 drinks which is the recommended level for men.
    B. No, because he is drinking vodka and moderate drinking only applies to beer and wine.
    C. No, his daily consumption is much less than what is considered moderate.
    D. No, because each of his drinks contains twice as much alcohol as a standard drink (1.5 oz. of distilled spirits) so he is drinking much more alcohol.

23. Do you think Steve is depressed, alcohol dependent, or both?   23.____
    A. Steve is depressed. His symptoms are typical of a depressive episode.
    B. Steve is alcohol dependent. His symptoms are typical of alcohol dependence.
    C. Steve is both depressed and alcohol dependent and should be evaluated and treated for both until one is ruled out.
    D. Steve is alcohol dependent and the symptoms of depression are the result of alcohol and will probably clear up after ninety days of treatment.

24. What types of treatment do you think Steve may need?   24.____
    A. Because of his depressive symptoms and physical withdrawal symptoms, Steve may need inpatient detox and monitoring. He should also attend AA or other 12-step meetings and receive pharmaco-therapy if necessary.
    B. After detox, Steve should be able to abstain from drinking and should not need follow-up care.
    C. Outpatient treatment is best because the least restrictive setting should always be used and Steve has a supportive family and a strong incentive to do well so that he can keep his job.

Question 25.

DIRECTIONS: Question 25 is based on the following passage.

Bryan is a school teacher, 37 years of age. He consumes alcohol about once a month. He has been reading about the beneficial effects of moderate drinking on cardiovascular disease and certain types of stroke. Before increasing alcohol consumption, he decides to discuss what and how much he should drink and the risks and benefits with his primary care provider. When asked about his family's history, he says his biological father may have had a drinking problem and gone to Alcoholics Anonymous (AA) but that he was raised by his mother and stepfather in a non-drinking household.

25. Should Bryan increase his alcohol consumption?   25.____
    A. Yes, he will need to increase his consumption to take advantage of the beneficial effects.
    B. No, because of his age, lack of history of other cardio-protective interventions and also because his biological father had an alcohol problem.
    C. Yes, after weighing the potential risks and benefits.
    D. None of the above

_____

KEY (CORRECT ANSWERS)

1.	C		11.	D
2.	A		12.	C
3.	D		13.	A
4.	D		14.	D
5.	D		15.	B
6.	B		16.	A
7.	C		17.	C
8.	C		18.	D
9.	C		19.	B
10.	B		20.	D

21.	B
22.	D
23.	C
24.	A
25.	B

_____

EXAMINATION SECTION
TEST 1

DIRECTIONS: Each question or incomplete statement is followed by several suggested answers or completions. Select the one that BEST answers the question or completes the statement. *PRINT THE LETTER OF THE CORRECT ANSWER IN THE SPACE AT THE RIGHT.*

Questions 1-13.

DIRECTIONS: Questions 1 through 13 are to be answered on the basis of the following information.

Sonny Burnett, a drug addict, is admitted to the hospital and is suspected of having hepatitis. The diagnosis of Type B hepatitis is confirmed, and Sonny is placed in a unit with other drug addicts. A decision to attempt a *cold turkey* withdrawal for Sonny is made by the health team.

1. Which of the following observations indicates that Sonny has recently had *a fix?*   1.____

    A.   Increased blood pressure
    B.   Fruity breath
    C.   Needle marks on his extremities
    D.   Constricted pupils

2. Which of the following statements should be included in the nurse's instructions to Sonny concerning his illness?   2.____

    A.   Treatment with hepatitis B immune globulin will provide you with immunity.
    B.   You have developed an immunity to viral hepatitis.
    C.   You will have a lifelong immunity to serum hepatitis.
    D.   You will always be more susceptible to serum hepatitis.

3. To prevent the spread of the disease to others, the nurse should place Sonny on _____ isolation precautions.   3.____

    A.   blood and body fluids
    B.   respiratory and body fluids
    C.   respiratory and enteric
    D.   enteric and blood

4. The nursing care plan includes expanding the range of interests of the clients in Sonny's group.
The MOST therapeutic initial approach would be to   4.____

    A.   accept the group's need to communicate in the addict's jargon
    B.   speak to the group about the harmful effects of drug abuse
    C.   support the group members in their need to discuss their habit
    D.   discourage the group from discussing drugs or having gutter talk

5. The symptoms that Sonny would MOST likely exhibit at the onset of *cold turkey* withdrawal are
   - A. weight loss, severe stomach cramps, and vomiting
   - B. muscular pain, anorexia, and diarrhea
   - C. diaphoresis, yawning, lacrimation, and sneezing
   - D. restlessness, insomnia, and increased blood pressure

5.____

6. Sonny asks the nurse how long he is going to suffer the withdrawal symptoms. The MOST accurate reply by the nurse would be that if you just started withdrawal, symptoms should begin in _____ hours, peak in _____, and subside in _____.
   - A. 4; 24 hours; 48 hours
   - B. 12; 36 hours; 72 hours
   - C. 24; 3 days; 5 days
   - D. 36; 5 days; 7 days

6.____

7. The MOST therapeutic action by the nurse during the peak phase of Sonny's withdrawal from heroin would be
   - A. providing adequate fluid intake
   - B. providing a supplementary diet
   - C. instituting convulsion precautions
   - D. administering prescribed sedation

7.____

8. Sonny's laboratory findings show a slight improvement, but he is suffering from appetite loss.
   To ensure adequate nutrition, the nurse should
   - A. request an order for intravenous fluid and vitamin therapy
   - B. weigh Sonny at least every second day and keep him informed of his weight changes
   - C. provide Sonny with small meals and high-protein beverages between meals
   - D. encourage ambulation to stimulate Sonny's appetit

8.____

9. Sonny was found with the following symptoms during his withdrawal from heroin. Which set of symptoms suggests a complication that would require IMMEDIATE nursing intervention?
   - A. Marked rise in temperature or blood pressure, or both
   - B. Anxiety, tremors, and depression
   - C. Nausea, vomiting, and diarrhea
   - D. Profuse diaphoresis, influenza symptoms, and chills

9.____

10. Sonny and the health care team discuss what type of environment he needs for best recovery from his drug problem and decide on a structured environment.
    Of the following characteristics of this environment, the one that will be of GREATEST basic benefit to Sonny is
    - A. having others tell him what to do
    - B. knowing what the rules are and what is expected of him
    - C. being protected from outside influences
    - D. learning more about the effects of drugs

10.____

11. Sonny, after noticing and being curious, asks the nurse why some of the clients are receiving methadone as a replacement for heroin.
The BEST reply by the nurse would be that this narcotic is given because it   11.____

    A. cannot be taken with other drugs
    B. is nonaddictive
    C. gives a euphoric feeling
    D. relieves withdrawal symptoms

12. Sonny asks the nurse why it is necessary for one to have a periodic urine test when taking methadone.
Which of the following would be the BEST reply by the nurse?   12.____

    A. We need to test the kidneys' threshold to methadone.
    B. Methadone irritates the kidneys, so we have to do a kidney function test.
    C. We test for drugs other than methadone.
    D. We have to determine the methadone dosage.

13. Sonny wants to know why heroin causes hepatitis.
The explanation by the nurse that would be MOST appropriate for Sonny is: 13.____

    A. Heroin reduces one's natural defenses
    B. Hepatitis is not caused by heroin
    C. Hepatitis is caused by a germ found on the skin
    D. Hepatitis is caused by using dirty needles

Questions 14-18.

DIRECTIONS: Questions 14 through 18 are to be answered on the basis of the following information.

Linda Carter, age 24, just got discharged from the hospital after being treated for substance abuse. She is addicted to alcohol and cocaine. She is now seeing Ms. Flores, the nurse at the local mental health center.

14. Ms. Flores plans to help Linda adjust to the activities of the community mental health center.
The FIRST action taken by the nurse should be to   14.____

    A. ask for a detailed history of threatened drug abuse
    B. assess her own feelings about the client's lack of control
    C. assign the client to a volunteer who also has had a drug problem
    D. introduce herself and state her objectives

15. Linda tells the group at the health center that her drinking was caused by her family, who all drank like fish. How should the nurse analyze this behavior?   15.____

    A. Linda's family was the cause of her drug use.
    B. Most users get addicted to drugs through their families.
    C. The behavior of most drug users is aggression turned outward.
    D. Linda does not take responsibility for her drug use.

16. Linda comes to the center with alcohol odor on her breath. The nurse should   16.____
    A. assign her to an Alcoholics Anonymous group meeting
    B. call her family to come and take her home
    C. ask her what happened to make her want a drink
    D. tell her that she cannot come to the center while drinking

17. Linda tells the nurse that she always felt she wasn't good enough, and with drugs she felt   17.____
    she was the greatest. The BEST plan of action for her at this time would be to
    A. suggest that she put trust in a supreme being
    B. offer recognition for accomplishing tasks
    C. encourage her to talk to others who have similar problems
    D. recommend that she live life one day at a time

18. Another important plan for the future that Linda and the nurse should make to help her   18.____
    overcome her addictive behavior is that she must
    A. not resume a relationship with her old drinking friends
    B. find a time-filling and gratifying occupation
    C. not attend any social gatherings without a chaperone
    D. move back into the protective environment of her family

Questions 19-28.

DIRECTIONS: Questions 19 through 28 are to be answered on the basis of the following information.

Burt Right, 28 years old, has a history of juvenile offenses, having an arrogant manner, always being a loner, and preferring to do things his own way. He can see no wrong in himself and no right in others.

Due to his aggressive behavior, he once got involved in a serious fight and got shot in the right leg. While Burt's physical condition has been improving, he continually demonstrates disruptive behavior. He has been arrogant and demanding.

19. After a psychiatric consultation, Burt is diagnosed as having antisocial behavior.   19.____
    Which problem exhibited by the client would be the MOST difficult for the staff to handle?
    A. Having problems in distinguishing true statements from lies
    B. Not being able to form a close relationship
    C. Being persistent in his antisocial behavior
    D. Not learning from experience

20. Burt is transferred to a psychiatric unit. During orientation, Burt is told of the rules and   20.____
    regulations of the unit. One day, he borrows another person's shampoo without permission. He says to the nurse, *It's not stealing when you borrow shampoo.*
    The nurse's BEST response in this situation is:
    A. Keep the shampoo; I will get more for the other patient.
    B. Give the client his shampoo back and tell him you are sorry

C. You will not be penalized; the rules do not include borrowing shampoo
D. The rule is, when you steal you will be penalized

21. When Burt is confronted about his unacceptable behavior toward others, the staff should expect him to

    A. become very angry
    B. accept the criticism
    C. show very little concern
    D. withdraw from others

21.____

22. The group which would probably provide the MOST therapeutic advice in the course of determining penalties for breaking the rules of the mental health unit would be the

    A. clients who live in the unit and have to abide by the rules
    B. lay people in the community who determine hospital policy
    C. members of the administrative group who determine the rules of the hospital
    D. members of the mental health professional staff who set the standards of the unit

22.____

23. Which approach by the nursing team would be MOST effective with Burt?

    A. Providing a nonstructured environment
    B. Being a part of the therapeutic community
    C. A one-to-one relationship
    D. Allowing Burt to direct his treatment

23.____

24. Burt appears to be very reliable, has excellent reasoning, is not reacting in an emotionally disturbed way, and his actions seem to be completely normal.
The nurse can BEST assess his behavior through obtaining

    A. Burt's cooperation and consent
    B. a series of psychological tests
    C. a detailed history from Burt
    D. his behavioral history from acquaintances

24.____

25. The health team has been observing Burt's interactions with members of his family.
Which behavior of the family would MOST likely contribute to Burt's illness?

    A. Being overprotective, hypochondriacal, symbiotic, and dependent
    B. Violence, indifference, rejection, and lack of predictability
    C. Using sexual provocation and being compulsive and rigid
    D. Setting goals too high, and thus making Burt feel guilty

25.____

26. The members of the staff have started having difficulty accepting Burt and have started criticizing him even when he has not broken a rule.
The PROBABLE reason for this nontherapeutic approach is that

    A. Burt's behavior is very destructive to others
    B. Burt's behavior is considered pathological
    C. Burt does not reinforce the staff for its efforts
    D. the staff can show Burt that inconsistency is not therapeutic

26.____

27. The nurse analyzing Burt's behavior recognizes that he is often in conflict with others   27.____
because he has

    A. disguised his deep feelings for others
    B. never learned group norms and loyalty
    C. reverted to regressive patterns of behavior
    D. lived his life in an asocial environment

28. Burt and his family have been in therapy for eight months. Burt is receiving therapy   28.____
through the hospital clinic.
In evaluating Burt's progress, the health team is most likely to observe that Burt shows
internalized acceptable behavior MOST often

    A. when interacting with the clients
    B. after talking to the nursing staff
    C. after visits with his family
    D. during the hourly sessions with his doctor

Questions 29-30.

DIRECTIONS: Questions 29 and 30 are to be answered on the basis of the following information.

    A client of yours is Jill Lebensfield, who is 30 years old. She was admitted because she
had attacked her neighbor with a knife as, according to her, the neighbor was unlawfully wire-
tapping her house. She continues to feel that others are spying on her.

29. Jill tells the nurse, *I'm not crazy; I don't belong here, my neighbor does.*   29.____
What behavior pattern is she using?

    A. Sociopathic   B. Aggressive
    C. Neurotic   D. Projective

30. Jill uses this behavior because   30.____

    A. she never learned to control her temper
    B. it is a secondary gain of aggressive behavior
    C. some aspects of her life are difficult to handle
    D. social-moral codes were never learned

KEY (CORRECT ANSWERS)

1.	D		16.	C
2.	C		17.	B
3.	A		18.	A
4.	D		19.	D
5.	C		20.	D
6.	B		21.	C
7.	A		22.	A
8.	C		23.	B
9.	A		24.	D
10.	B		25.	B
11.	D		26.	C
12.	C		27.	B
13.	D		28.	A
14.	B		29.	D
15.	D		30.	C

TEST 2

DIRECTIONS: Each question or incomplete statement is followed by several suggested answers or completions. Select the one that BEST answers the question or completes the statement. *PRINT THE LETTER OF THE CORRECT ANSWER IN THE SPACE AT THE RIGHT.*

Questions 1-11.

DIRECTIONS: Questions 1 through 11 are to be answered on the basis of the following information.

Norman Bates, 24 years old, is brought to the emergency mental health center by his family. He had furiously tried to attack his mother. For the last 6 months, since graduating from college, he has not been able to find employment, and most of the time he sits and stares into space. On admission, he appears dazed and speaks incoherently.

1.   The nurse observes that Mr. Bates sits alone in the dayroom staring at the floor. His clothes are disheveled, and his hair and beard are unkempt. She approaches him and introduces herself as his primary nurse.
     Which statement would be MOST appropriate by the nurse at this time?

     A.   There is a meeting of all new clients and I will introduce you.
     B.   I will sit with you for 10 minutes. You don't have to talk.
     C.   This is the hour for occupational therapy. I will go with you.
     D.   If you care to, you may go to your room. You had a difficult night.

1.____

2.   The nurse observes Mr. Bates sitting alone. He is staring into space, smiling, and moving his lips as if talking to someone.
     How should the nurse approach him?

     A.   What do you see when you stare into space?
     B.   You must not sit by yourself; you will hear voices.
     C.   Tell me what the voices are telling you.
     D.   You were moving your lips, but made no sound.

2.____

3.   Mr. Bates tells the nurse that he hears voices telling him he is a good person.
     The MOST accurate reply by the nurse would be:

     A.   A stimulating environment can enhance one's senses and cause hallucinations.
     B.   You have an overactive imagination that makes up for a dull existence.
     C.   There are unconscious feelings breaking into your consciousness.
     D.   There must be some pathology to the sensory organ receptors or nerves.

3.____

4.   Mr. Bates asks the nurse when the best time to try to control the voices would be.
     Which reply would be MOST accurate?
     _____ the voices.

     A.   When you are actively hearing
     B.   When you are not hearing
     C.   When you are waiting to hear
     D.   Immediately after hearing

4.____

5. Mr. Bates tells the nurse, *You have a time to contact the individual.* The nurse recognizes that this is speech that has meaning only for the client in his primitive thoughts. What type of speech is this?

    A. Word salad   B. Magical thinking
    C. Looseness of association   D. Neologisms

5.____

6. Mr. Bates asks the nurse to give him an example of his behavior that the doctor called *delusions of reference.* Which reply by the nurse would be ACCURATE?

    A. The room is wired by the police, who want to get me.
    B. My body is disintegrating into a mass of jelly.
    C. I'm the prince of Wales; my name is Charles.
    D. The conversations and actions of others are always concerning me.

6.____

7. The nurse tells Mr. Bates that the long-term goal for the nurse/client therapeutic sessions is to help him

    A. accept his behavior and not feel guilty
    B. learn to communicate in a less symbolic way
    C. understand the reason for his sick behavior
    D. learn new skills so that he can find employment

7.____

8. After several weeks of daily therapeutic sessions, Mr. Bates tells the nurse, *You are like everyone else; you don't understand me – you are pushing.*
How should the nurse reply?

    A. Do you feel that I have been pushing you too fast?
    B. Not being understood must be very difficult.
    C. Who is this everyone else I remind you of?
    D. Maybe we should find someone else to replace me.

8.____

9. Mr. Bates asks the nurse why so many clients return to the hospital after being discharged.
The MAIN reason for this revolving-door syndrome is

    A. families and the community reject the client
    B. the client refuses to return for follow-up care in the community
    C. the client cannot find suitable employment
    D. a symbiotic relationship has developed with the staff

9.____

10. The nurse and Mr. Bates are ready to plan for his participation in groups.
Before making this plan, it should be considered whether he

    A. is accepted by other clients on the unit
    B. is ready to be discharged from the hospital
    C. can tolerate the nurse without stress
    D. still needs the nurse's support

10.____

11. A week before his discharge, Mr. Bates and the nurse go on a shopping trip.
The MAIN objective of this activity is to

    A. boost Mr. Bates' self-esteem by providing diversional activity in the community
    B. give Mr. Bates an opportunity to buy some clothes

11.____

C. assist Mr. Bates in implementing some skills he learned in the hospital
D. condition Mr. Bates toward acceptable behavior in the community

Questions 12-30.

DIRECTIONS: Questions 12 through 30 are to be answered on the basis of the following information.

Bobby Briggs, age 20, has been hospitalized for 14 days with compound fractures of the right tibia and fibula resulting from a motorcycle accident. After closed reduction of the fractures, he is placed in traction. His personality evaluation indicates that he is a shy, introspective person who keeps to himself and never talks unless asked a direct question. He has had no visitors.

12. Bobby's nurse assesses his emotional problem.
The nurse understands that, at his age, a PRIMARY developmental task is to

    12.____

A. have a sense of self and extended self in an intimate relationship
B. seek to become a part of a group with a sense of belonging to this group
C. have identified life's goals such as occupational and marital choices
D. gain feelings of self-worth as a result of appraisals from significant others

13. The nurse observes that Bobby appears very insecure.
The MOST effective nursing action in helping to alleviate Bobby's insecurity would be to

    13.____

A. allow him freedom to do what he wants
B. plan a consistent staff approach based on his needs
C. provide for his physical and emotional needs
D. assign someone to be with him until his anxiety subsides

14. The nurse understands that Bobby's withdrawn behavior is MOST likely due to the fact that

    14.____

A. there is a constant need for approval, yet he resents it
B. he has identified with the parent who lacks superego control
C. he has received too much protection from significant others
D. interpersonal relationships become a source of anxiet

15. The nurse also understands that Bobby's behavior is a defense, because the world of reality is painful for him. Which behavior should the nurse observe to confirm this?

    15.____

A. He avoids relationships by staying at a safe and familiar level of functioning.
B. His emotions have created visceral changes and he has repressed his emotions.
C. He can admit no fault in himself or any virtue in others.
D. He is preoccupied with a sense of self-depreciation and self-reproach.

16. The nurse has planned a series of interviews with Bobby.
The nurse should place the chair _____ from the client, to provide an appropriate space.

    16.____

A. 4 to 8 inches
C. 18 inches to 4 feet
B. 8 to 24 inches
D. 4 to 8 feet

17. The nurse understands that at this distance the nurse and client are more comfortable because

    A. the voice can be kept at a whisper
    B. fine details of the other person are lost
    C. they can touch one another without reaching
    D. vision and perception are not distorted

17.____

18. The nurse makes an appointment with Bobby to talk to him daily for approximately 30 minutes.
The nurse's PRIMARY goal in arranging these meetings is to

    A. aid Bobby with his socializing problem by socializing with him
    B. assist in identifying his problems in a one-to-one relationship
    C. help have a feeling that others in the environment care
    D. determine from Bobby why he is so withdrawn and has no friends

18.____

19. After being introduced, Bobby does not acknowledge the nurse's presence.
The nurse should know that

    A. admission to a new environment causes him to withdraw
    B. he needs rest if proper healing is to take place
    C. the accident may also have caused some brain injury
    D. rejection of interpersonal relationships is part of his defense

19.____

20. The FIRST short-term goal for the nurse to establish as a nursing care need of Bobby should be to

    A. establish and maintain the client's contact with reality
    B. provide for trust and security in the nurse/client relationship
    C. initiate and develop the nurse/client relationship
    D. encourage and support the client's interactions with others

20.____

21. At an early session, Bobby complains of discomfort in his lower back.
What action by the nurse would BEST meet Bobby's needs?

    A. Give him simple instructions for isometric exercises for the back.
    B. Give him his prn medication of Tylenol, 1000 mg.
    C. Give him a back rub while he raises his hip.
    D. Ask him when he had his last bowel movement.

21.____

22. The nurse implements nursing care to alleviate Bobby's back pain because

    A. physical touching will alleviate pain and also provide trust and security needed
    B. lack of bowel movement can cause pressure on the lower back
    C. isometric exercises will strengthen muscles and prevent atrophy
    D. Tylenol reduces pain caused by muscle spasms

22.____

23. Bobby tells the nurse that he has always liked to be alone. He states, *You know, the best company is my own.*
Which reply by the nurse would BEST expand his experience?

    A. You have a great deal of self-confidence, don't you?
    B. Are you saying you never enjoy the company of others?

23.____

C. Tell me how it makes you feel to be with others.
D. You will miss a lot of life by being a loner.

24. Although Bobby answers direct questions, there are long periods of silence. The nurse understands that Bobby is using this silence because he is

    A. thinking of what to say
    B. clarifying his thoughts
    C. severely depressed
    D. uncomfortable with others

24.____

25. The nurse can BEST break the silence with Bobby by saying:

    A. If I'm upsetting you, I'll be back later
    B. It must be difficult to talk to strangers
    C. What are you thinking about?
    D. Do these sessions with me make you nervous?

25.____

26. The nurse observes that Bobby cracks his knuckles whenever he is anxious. Which nursing action would be MOST therapeutic?

    A. Give him something to do with his hands so he will be occupied.
    B. Ask the physician to prescribe a mild tranquilizer for him.
    C. Explain to Bobby that this behavior will make his hands arthritic.
    D. Assess what causes this behavior and take steps to lessen his discomfort.

26.____

27. At another session, Bobby tells the nurse that his brother was to blame for the motorcycle accident. He states that if his brother hadn't sold it to him, he wouldn't be in this fix today.
The nurse understands that this statement reflects

    A. avoidance of a close relationship with his brother
    B. an impression that a different cycle would have been safer
    C. dislike of his brother who sold a defective cycle
    D. feelings of failure that he attributes to his brother

27.____

28. After Bobby made the statement blaming his brother for the accident, the nurse should reply:

    A. What do you and your family do for pleasure when you are together?
    B. This must be a difficult time for you. How did the accident happen?
    C. You feel that your brother sold you an inferior bike.
    D. It must be difficult for you being in pain, while your brother is not.

28.____

29. Bobby's health condition has improved.
The observation by the nurse that indicates that Bobby's emotional health has also improved is that he

    A. is able to talk about his problem and not withdraw
    B. gives the staff a box of chocolate for helping him
    C. tells the nurse he can work on his problems alone
    D. discontinues the sessions with the nurse therapist

29.____

30. Which referral group would be MOST beneficial for Bobby at the time he leaves the hospital?   30.____

    A.   Group of people who have problems communicating
    B.   Safety driving school for motorcyclists
    C.   Public health department for follow-up care
    D.   Encounter group where Bobby will be forced to look at his behavior

―――――――

KEY (CORRECT ANSWERS)

1.	D		16.	C
2.	B		17.	D
3.	C		18.	B
4.	C		19.	D
5.	A		20.	C
6.	D		21.	C
7.	B		22.	A
8.	C		23.	C
9.	B		24.	D
10.	C		25.	B
11.	D		26.	D
12.	A		27.	D
13.	B		28.	B
14.	D		29.	A
15.	A		30.	C

―――――――

EXAMINATION SECTION
TEST 1

DIRECTIONS: Each question or incomplete statement is followed by several suggested answers or completions. Select the one that BEST answers the question or completes the statement. *PRINT THE LETTER OF THE CORRECT ANSWER IN THE SPACE AT THE RIGHT.*

1. Which of the following symptoms, by itself, would NOT signify that a person receiving treatment for alcoholism might undergo a difficult period of withdrawal?

    A.   Previous history of seizures or delirium tremens
    B.   Ulcers or gastritis
    C.   Irritability or depression
    D.   Elevated blood pressure or pulse

1._____

2. In general, the format and direction of treatment for alcoholics and people dependent upon drugs should

    A.   differ in intensity according to the progression of the addiction
    B.   be flexible enough not to interfere with the patient's normal living patterns
    C.   begin with immediate isolation
    D.   remain the same for all patients

2._____

3. Which of the following words is NOT typically used to describe the disease of alcoholism?

    A.   Chronic
    C.   Primary
    B.   Nonfatal
    D.   Hereditary

3._____

4. Each of the following symptoms characterizes stage one in an alcoholic subject's withdrawal process EXCEPT

    A.   auditory hallucinations
    C.   hand tremors
    B.   loss of appetite
    D.   diarrhea

4._____

5. During the initial stages of recovery, which of the following vitamin supplements is NOT usually among the most important for the typically malnourished alcoholic subject?

    A.   Zinc
    C.   B-complex
    B.   Calcium
    D.   Vitamin C

5._____

6. What is the term for the point in recovery treatment that marks the clearest turning point, and signals that the subject has escaped immediate danger?

    A.   Submission
    C.   Surrender
    B.   Substitution
    D.   Synchronization

6._____

7. As a rule, _____ should always be excluded from the team making an intervention into an addicted person's life.

    A.   staff members of a treatment facility
    B.   people with abuse or addiction problems
    C.   the addicted person's professional superiors
    D.   members of the religious community

7._____

8. Approximately what percentage of untreated alcoholics will eventually experience delirium tremens?

    A. 10%   B. 20%   C. 30%   D. 40%

8.___

9. Each of the following is considered to be one of the essential elements in subduing an addiction EXCEPT

    A. total abstinence
    B. firm but compassionate care
    C. nutritional repair
    D. vigorous physical exercise

9.___

10. Which of the following stages in the progression to freedom from addiction is considered to be the foundation on which all other elements are dependent?

    A. Spiritual well-being   B. Mental well-being
    C. Total abstinence   D. Physical well-being

10.___

11. Which of the following is a sign of early-stage addiction in an adolescent?

    A. Increase in tolerance   B. Legal problems
    C. Changes in appearance   D. Buying drugs

11.___

12. Which of the following is NOT normally included in the description of a *typical* alcoholic in the early stages of treatment?

    A. Withdrawn   B. Suspicious
    C. Talks loudly   D. Poorly groomed

12.___

13. Which of the following is considered to be an internal enabler for abuse or addiction?

    A. Modeling of use by parents
    B. Approval of use by peers
    C. The removal of deterrent consequences
    D. Rationalization of use

13.___

14. Approximately what percentage of alcoholics are heavy caffeine drinkers?

    A. 0-10%   B. 10-15%   C. 45-50%   D. 90-95%

14.___

15. Good addiction treatment facilities have all of the following characteristics in common EXCEPT

    A. reliance on psychotherapy
    B. family involvement
    C. introduction and participation in AA or related groups
    D. occupational guidance

15.___

16. Which factor in an individual's predisposition to addiction is related to the biological differences between addicts and non-addicts?

    A. Genetic   B. Constitutional
    C. Psychological   D. Sociocultural

16.___

17. Typically, no detoxifying agents or drugs are used for the detoxification period during treatment for addiction to   17.____

    A. alcohol   B. opiates   C. cocaine   D. valium

18. Which of the following elements is considered to be unique to teenage alcoholism or addiction?   18.____

    A. Self-centeredness
    B. Peer pressure
    C. Rebelliousness
    D. Fear of life without drugs

19. A component of a comprehensive addiction treatment program that is included in the category of evaluation and assessment is   19.____

    A. treating physiological crises
    B. family therapy
    C. addiction screening
    D. stress reduction

20. The middle stages of alcoholism are often characterized by the onset of   20.____

    A. a progressive increase in drinking
    B. financial dependence
    C. guilty feelings
    D. alcohol-related arrests

21. Which of the following unconscious defense mechanisms, used by an addicted person, is characterized by blaming others for behaviors and consequences?   21.____

    A. Denial   B. Minimization
    C. Rationalization   D. Projection

22. Which of the following *leverages,* or inducements for voluntary submission to treatment, would be LEAST appropriate for use by members of an intervention team?   22.____

    A. Termination of employment
    B. Threat of divorce
    C. Threat of institutionalization
    D. Termination of friendship

23. Which of the following is NOT considered to be one of the primary goals in a structured detoxification process?   23.____

    A. Helping ease the pain associated with withdrawal
    B. Allowing the symptoms of withdrawal to run their natural course
    C. Correcting underlying medical problems or malnutrition
    D. Preparing patient for abstinence without dependence on other drugs

24. The _____ is ALWAYS a mistake on the part of treatment staff while the patient is going through the detoxification process.   24.____

    A. administration of narcotic sedatives
    B. prolonged isolation of the subject
    C. attempt to induce the subject's acknowledgement of his/her addiction
    D. liberal administration of multivitamin supplements

25. The enabling behaviors MOST likely to be practiced by the addicted person's family   25.____
    members in the intermediate stages of addiction are

    A.   cooperation and collaboration
    B.   protecting and shielding
    C.   codependence and cohabitation
    D.   control and guilt

_____

KEY (CORRECT ANSWERS)

1.	C	11.	A
2.	D	12.	D
3.	B	13.	D
4.	A	14.	D
5.	A	15.	A
6.	C	16.	B
7.	B	17.	C
8.	A	18.	B
9.	D	19.	C
10.	C	20.	C

21.	D
22.	C
23.	B
24.	C
25.	D

_____

TEST 2

DIRECTIONS: Each question or incomplete statement is followed by several suggested answers or completions. Select the one that BEST answers the question or completes the statement. *PRINT THE LETTER OF THE CORRECT ANSWER IN THE SPACE AT THE RIGHT.*

1. Recurring withdrawal symptoms are LEAST common during the treatment for _____ addiction.　　　　　　　　　　　　　　　　　　　　　　　　　　　　　1.____

    A. alcohol   B. valium   C. amphetamine   D. cocaine

2. The normalization process during the posttreatment restructuring phase of recovery treatment includes　　　　　　　　　　　　　　　　　　　　　　　　　　　2.____

    A. increasing self-esteem through feedback
    B. learning communication skills
    C. a physical exercise program
    D. implementation of a healthy diet

3. Stage three in an alcoholic's withdrawal process is characterized by　　　　　　3.____

    A. delirium tremens   B. seizures
    C. auditory hallucinations   D. insomnia

4. The characteristic of an addicted person's recovery illustrated by the person's acknowledgement of his/her addiction is termed　　　　　　　　　　　　　　　　　　4.____

    A. surrender   B. acceptance   C. admission   D. restitution

5. During the early stages of recovery treatment, which of the following characteristics of a subject's expression or demeanor is usually NOT a cause for worry on the part of the treatment staff?　　　　　　　　　　　　　　　　　　　　　　　　　　　5.____

    A. Boredom   B. Anxiety   C. Aloofness   D. Arrogance

6. Which of the following steps should be taken FIRST by friends/family members who want to practice intervention in a person's addiction?　　　　　　　　　　　　　　6.____

    A. Devising a treatment plan
    B. Confronting the addicted person
    C. Getting help for the person's family
    D. Asking others for help

7. An addicted person who would require one of the less intense levels of recovery treatment and care would PROBABLY　　　　　　　　　　　　　　　　　　　　7.____

    A. have chronic psychiatric problems
    B. lack family or social support
    C. already be resigned to treatment
    D. have family members who were also addicted

8. The percentage of people with psychotic disorders among the alcoholic population is _____ that of the general population.　　　　　　　　　　　　　　　　　8.____

    A. half as much as   B. no different than
    C. one a half times as much as   D. twice as much as

9. A recovering addict will typically experience the GREATEST risk of relapse during 9.___

    A. detoxification
    B. the first six months of treatment
    C. the second six months of treatment
    D. late stage recovery

10. The depressant which usually carries the GREATEST potential for dependency or abuse is 10.___

    A. valium   B. librium   C. halcion   D. seconal

11. Each of the following is considered to be a crucial element in the detoxification process EXCEPT 11.___

    A. stimulation   B. security   C. supplements   D. sedation

12. Which of the addiction risk factors is considered to be the MOST influential? 12.___

    A. Hereditary   B. Behavioral   C. Demographic   D. Psychiatric

13. The component of a, comprehensive addiction treatment program that is included in the category of medical and psychiatric management is 13.___

    A. detoxification   B. recreation and leisure
    C. group therapy   D. relapse prevention training

14. Which of the following is NOT typically a characteristic more pronounced in female alcoholics than in males? 14.___

    A. Greater degree of guilt
    B. More likely to feel locked into unhealthy relationships
    C. More likely to use illegal drugs
    D. More difficulty dealing with feelings of inadequacy

15. The information needed first to determine whether a person is addicted, and to which all other factors are secondary considerations, are the 15.___

    A. results of the person's physical examination
    B. person's performance level at home and on the job
    C. person's overall pattern of alcohol or drug use
    D. person's family medical history

16. Which of the following is considered part of the necessary treatment for an alcoholic subject who has entered stage one of the withdrawal process? 16.___

    A. Sedation
    B. Well-lit room
    C. Constant medical supervision
    D. Intravenous administration of fluid supplements

17. Mood-altering drugs are capable of each of the following EXCEPT 17.____

   A. causing psychiatric symptoms of varying intensity
   B. masking existing psychiatric symptoms and disorders
   C. curing certain psychiatric disorders
   D. initiate or worsen existing psychiatric disorders

18. When initially questioning a subject about his or her use of alcohol or drugs, the ques-   18.____
   tioner should avoid asking, until the later stages of treatment, whether

   A. the subject drinks or uses drugs
   B. the subject has experienced any trouble related to the use of drugs or alcohol
   C. the subject feels any guilt about his/her use of drugs or alcohol
   D. any friends or relatives have had problems with drugs or alcohol

19. Elderly alcoholics typically differ from others in that they are MORE likely to 19.____

   A. deny their addiction
   B. combine their alcoholism with over-the-counter drug addiction
   C. begin their drinking in social settings
   D. become afflicted with alcoholism

20. The normalization process during the mature recovery phase of treatment includes 20.____

   A. personality restructuring
   B. introduction of normal sleep patterns
   C. personality growth
   D. stress reduction techniques

21. Which of the following is a sign that an adolescent has entered the intermediate stage of   21.____
   addiction?

   A. Denial
   B. Abuse as an act of defiance
   C. Increasing tolerance
   D. First blackouts

22. Which of the following is NOT one of the benefits associated with the use of sedatives   22.____
   during a subject's withdrawal period?

   A. Reduces fear of new surroundings and circumstances
   B. Shortens the time needed for detoxification
   C. Reduces likelihood of premature departure
   D. Prevents progression of withdrawal symptoms into advanced stages

23. Which stage in the progression to freedom from addiction is considered to be the inter-   23.____
   mediate level of recovery?

   A. Spiritual well-being   B. Mental well-being
   C. Total abstinence   D. Physical well-being

24. Each of the following symptoms typically signify that a drinker has progressed to the advanced stages of the alcoholic disease EXCEPT

    A. lack of attention to hygiene
    B. increased tolerance for alcohol
    C. morning drinking
    D. alcohol-related accidents

24.____

25. What is the typical percentage of alcoholic people entering treatment programs who will require the use of sedatives during withdrawal?

    A. 1-10%   B. 10-20%   C. 20-30%   D. 30-40%

25.____

KEY (CORRECT ANSWERS)

1.	A		11.	A
2.	A		12.	A
3.	A		13.	A
4.	C		14.	C
5.	B		15.	C
6.	D		16.	B
7.	C		17.	C
8.	B		18.	C
9.	B		19.	B
10.	D		20.	A

21.	A
22.	B
23.	B
24.	B
25.	C

EXAMINATION SECTION
TEST 1

DIRECTIONS: Each question or incomplete statement is followed by several suggested answers or completions. Select the one that BEST answers the question or completes the statement. *PRINT THE LETTER OF THE CORRECT ANSWER IN THE SPACE AT THE RIGHT.*

1. Which of the following is NOT an inherent characteristic of addiction?   1.____

    A. Tolerance changes
    C. Physiological dependence
    B. Dissolution of relationships
    D. Loss of self-control

2. Which type of factor in an individual's predisposition to addiction has the GREATEST   2.____
potential to increase the risk of addiction after exposure to a substance?

    A. Genetic   B. Constitutional   C. Psychological   D. Sociocultural

3. The enabling behavior MOST likely practiced by the addicted person's family members in   3.____
the early stages of addiction are

    A. cooperation and collaboration
    C. codependence and cohabitation
    B. protecting and shielding
    D. control and guilt

4. When making initial inquiries about an addicted person's drug or alcohol abuse patterns   4.____
and history, which of the following is probably the LEAST reliable?

    A. Information provided by the subject's friends and relatives
    B. Information provided by the patient or subject
    C. Medical histories of subject's family members
    D. Subject's medical record

5. Which of the following is NOT one of the physical factors influencing addiction?   5.____

    A. Heredity
    C. Metabolism
    B. Brain chemistry
    D. Race

6. In a recovery treatment center, which of the following behaviors or characteristics gives   6.____
the STRONGEST indication that a subject is still addicted?

    A. Feeling caged or jailed
    C. Nervousness
    B. Mood swings
    D. Depression

7. Which of the following is NOT true of *leverages* used by members of an intervention   7.____
team to induce an addicted person to voluntarily submit to treatment?
They should

    A. only be used as a last resort
    B. not be carried out if they will result in isolating the addicted person
    C. be agreed upon and supported by every member of the intervention team
    D. not be threatened unless they will definitely be implemented

8. What percentage of untreated alcoholics will eventually experience seizures?   8.____

     A. 5-15%   B. 20-30%   C. 40-50%   D. 55-75%

9. Which of the following is a sign that an adolescent has entered the late stages of addiction?   9.____

     A. Impulsiveness   B. Decrease in attention span
     C. Chronic depression   D. Denial

10. The type of drug dependency requiring the longest treatment time is USUALLY caused by   10.____

     A. alcohol   B. amphetamines
     C. opiates or cocaine   D. hallucinogens

11. Which of the following is NOT one of the primary factors in the formula that results in addiction?   11.____

     A. Drug effect   B. Social constraints
     C. Predisposition for abuse   D. Enabling factors

12. Drugs sometimes used in detoxification and which occupy a person's opiate-receptor sites without creating an accompanying sense of euphoria or loss of consciousness are   12.____

     A. opioids   B. opiates
     C. agonists   D. placebos

13. The normalization process during the late recovery phase of treatment includes   13.____

     A. increasingly sobriety-centered lifestyle
     B. discussion of drug hunger
     C. personality growth
     D. stress reduction techniques

14. Which of the following unconscious defense mechanisms, used by an addicted person, is characterized by partial awareness of the severity of the addiction?   14.____

     A. Denial   B. Minimization
     C. Rationalization   D. Isolation

15. The characteristic of an addicted person's recovery illustrated by the person's attempt to repair the relationships damaged by his/her addiction is   15.____

     A. fellowship   B. surrender
     C. admission   D. restitution

16. Which of the following is a sign that a drinker has entered the late stages of alcoholism?   16.____

     A. Progressive increase in drinking
     B. Broken promises to friends and family
     C. Personality changes
     D. Malnutrition

17. An alcoholic subject is said to have entered stage four of the withdrawal process if he or she experiences

    A. seizures
    B. delirium tremens
    C. vomiting
    D. hallucinations

17._____

18. Which of the following unconscious defense mechanisms, used by an addicted person, is characterized by an avoidance of feelings through focusing on logic?

    A. Rationalization
    B. Intellectualization
    C. Repression
    D. Projection

18._____

19. Measuring from the starting point of detoxification, what is typically the amount of time required for a recovering person to regain the level of health and well-being associated with his/her pre-addiction lifestyle?

    A. 6 months
    B. 1 year
    C. 18 months
    D. 3 years

19._____

20. A characteristic that typically differentiates teenage alcoholism from adult alcoholism is that teenagers

    A. are more likely to explain that they drink to celebrate or be sociable
    B. have a more difficult time with recovery
    C. claim drinking as an escape from life's problems
    D. sustain less physiological damage

20._____

21. Which type of recovery treatment is reserved for the most advanced cases of addiction?

    A. Day treatment
    B. Residential treatment
    C. Inpatient hospitalization
    D. Partial hospitalization

21._____

22. The use of which opiate drug typically carries the LOWEST risk for dependency or abuse?

    A. Percodan
    B. Methadone
    C. Codeine
    D. Demerol

22._____

23. What is the APPROXIMATE mortality rate for alcoholic patients who suffer from delirium tremens?

    A. Zero
    B. 1-10%
    C. 10-20%
    D. 20-30%

23._____

24. Addiction is a process influenced primarily by each of the following EXCEPT

    A. factors relating to the individual user
    B. various social factors
    C. factors relating to specific physiological health concerns
    D. factors relating to the drug being used

24._____

25. Which of the following statements about alcoholism is NOT true?

    A. Children of alcoholics often learn alcoholic behavior from their parents.
    B. Divorce, loss of a job, death of a loved one, and other life traumas can cause alcoholism.
    C. Alcoholism is often a symptom of larger psychological problems.
    D. An alcoholic in the throes of the disease drinks to avoid self-destruction.

25._____

KEY (CORRECT ANSWERS)

1.	B	11.	B
2.	A	12.	C
3.	B	13.	C
4.	B	14.	B
5.	D	15.	D
6.	A	16.	D
7.	B	17.	B
8.	A	18.	B
9.	C	19.	C
10.	C	20.	A

21.	C
22.	C
23.	C
24.	C
25.	D

———————

TEST 2

DIRECTIONS: Each question or incomplete statement is followed by several suggested answers or completions. Select the one that BEST answers the question or completes the statement. *PRINT THE LETTER OF THE CORRECT ANSWER IN THE SPACE AT THE RIGHT.*

1. Age, peers, and status are examples of _____ factors in an individual's predisposition to addiction.

   A. genetic   B. constitutional   C. psychological   D. sociocultural

   1.____

2. How many days should an alcoholic subject's detoxification process typically last?

   A. 1-10   B. 10-20   C. 20-30   D. 30-40

   2.____

3. Which of the following is NOT true of the confrontation that takes place between members of an intervention team and an addicted person?
   It must

   A. be rehearsed by all team members together
   B. involve quick-thinking people who can formulate responses to unanticipated statements
   C. involve people from a variety of the addicted person's life experiences
   D. be rigidly planned and structured

   3.____

4. What is the characteristic of an addicted person's recovery illustrated by the person's expression of willingness to accept the help of treatment staff in the recovery process?

   A. Surrender   B. Acceptance   C. Fellowship   D. Restitution

   4.____

5. In the early stages of an addicted or alcoholic person's recovery, the process of nutritional repair should include each of the following EXCEPT

   A. three good meals a day
   B. total elimination of caffeine intake
   C. three nutritious snacks a day
   D. increasing the amount of sugars in the diet

   5.____

6. Which of the following stages in the progression to freedom from addiction is considered to be the final stage, at which recovery is complete?

   A. Spiritual well-being   B. Mental well-being
   C. Total abstinence   D. Physical well-being

   6.____

7. The FIRST goal of recovery treatment is to remedy _____ damage to the addicted person.

   A. social   B. psychological   C. physical   D. spiritual

   7.____

8. Which of the following steps should be taken LAST by friends/family members who want to practice intervention in a person's addiction?

   A. Devising a treatment plan
   B. Confronting the addicted person
   C. Getting help for the person's family
   D. Asking others for help

   8.____

9. Each of the following is a disadvantage associated with the use of sedatives during an   9.____
   alcoholic subject's withdrawal EXCEPT that it

   A. increases suspicion and paranoia
   B. conflicts with the *abstinence* goal of detoxification
   C. lengthens the detoxification period
   D. interferes with the subject's alertness and early participation in treatment

10. Which of the following symptoms does addiction MOST commonly share with other   10.____
    chronic, debilitating diseases?

    A. Central nervous system damage
    B. Seizures
    C. Denial
    D. Physiological damage

11. An addicted person who would require one of the more intense levels of recovery treat-   11.____
    ment and care would PROBABLY have

    A. minor withdrawal symptoms
    B. family members who attend Al-Anon
    C. already be resigned to treatment
    D. already attempted recovery at least once and failed

12. The enabling behavior MOST likely practiced by the addicted person's family members in   12.____
    the advanced stages of addiction is

    A. cooperation   B. protecting
    C. codependence   D. guilt

13. Which of the following is NOT a symptom associated with stage two in an alcoholic sub-   13.____
    ject's withdrawal process?

    A. Rapid heartbeat   B. Hand tremors
    C. Insomnia   D. Seizures

14. During intervention, participants on the intervention team should avoid describing to the   14.____
    addicted person

    A. concerns for the addicted person's health
    B. observed examples of addiction-related incidents
    C. observed consequences of addiction-related incidents
    D. personal assessment of emotional damage inflicted upon the addicted person's
       relations

15. During recovery, a subject sometimes becomes dependent on a drug that has the same   15.____
    relative effects on the central nervous system as the drug for which the subject is being
    treated.
    This is known specifically as

    A. substitution   B. cross-addiction
    C. surrender   D. submission

16. During an intervention, which of the following types of statements should be offered to   16.____
the addicted person by members of the intervention team?

    A. Generalized comments   B. Judgments
    C. Observations   D. Opinions

17. Past failures, emotional trauma, and personality defects are examples of _____ factors   17.____
in an individual's predisposition to addiction.

    A. genetic   B. constitutional
    C. psychological   D. sociocultural

18. The normalization process during the restabilization phase of recovery treatment   18.____
includes

    A. introducing external motivations for recovery
    B. personality restructuring
    C. personality growth
    D. stress reduction techniques

19. Which characteristic typically differs between female and male alcoholics?   19.____

    A. Age
    B. Rate of advancement through addictive stages
    C. Likelihood of concurrent addiction to prescription drugs
    D. Professional status

20. Each of the following is an important factor determining the overall effects of addiction on   20.____
a family EXCEPT

    A. the type of substance used
    B. the sex of addicted parent
    C. existing feelings of nonaddicted family members toward the addicted
    D. where and when substances are used

21. The component of a comprehensive addiction treatment program that is included in the   21.____
category of psychosocial rehabilitation is

    A. social assessment   B. treating medical problems
    C. random drug screenings   D. detoxification

22. Each of the following is considered a warning sign for the onset of alcoholism's early   22.____
stages EXCEPT

    A. alcohol-related problems   B. hiding bottles
    C. changes in drinking patterns   D. preoccupation with alcohol

23. If sedatives are to be used by a subject during the alcoholic withdrawal period, APPROX-   23.____
IMATELY how long is the recommended period for their use?

    A. For the first overnight period
    B. For the first three or four days
    C. Until the subject does not appear to require sedation
    D. Throughout the entire period of detoxification

24. Which of the following is NOT one of the psychological factors influencing addiction? 24.____

    A. Coping mechanisms   B. Denial
    C. Tolerance changes   D. Reinforcing factors

25. The characteristic of an addicted person's recovery illustrated by the person's acknowl- 25.____
edgement of his/her individual responsibility for recovery is termed

    A. surrender   B. acceptance
    C. fellowship   D. admission

———

KEY (CORRECT ANSWERS)

1.	D		11.	D
2.	A		12.	C
3.	B		13.	D
4.	A		14.	D
5.	D		15.	B
6.	A		16.	C
7.	C		17.	C
8.	B		18.	D
9.	A		19.	C
10.	C		20.	A

21.	C
22.	B
23.	B
24.	C
25.	B

———

PHARMACOLOGY

EXAMINATION SECTION
TEST 1

DIRECTIONS: Each question or incomplete statement is followed by several suggested answers or completions. Select the one that BEST answers the question or completes the statement. *PRINT THE LETTER OF THE CORRECT ANSWER IN THE SPACE AT THE RIGHT.*

1.   The following properties common to all drugs of abuse are that they   1.____

    A.   have the ability to produce physical dependence
    B.   cause rapid development of tolerance
    C.   have the ability to elicit withdrawal symptoms upon discontinuance
    D.   have the ability to change one's mood and sensory perceptions
    E.   none of the above

2.   Which of the following antibiotics should be considered the drug of choice in the treat-   2.____
ment of infection caused by a penicillinase-producing staphylococcus?

    A.   Neomycin   B.   Ampicillin
    C.   Tetracycline   D.   Penicillin V
    E.   Dicloxacillin

3.   Which of the following antibiotics may be crossallergenic with penicillin?   3.____

    A.   Neomycin   B.   Cephalexin
    C.   Clindamycin   D.   Erythromycin
    E.   All of the above

4.   Which of the following is TRUE regarding the mechanism of action of local anesthetics?   4.____
They

    A.   usually maintain the nerve membrane in a state of hyperpolarization
    B.   prevent the generation of a nerve action potential
    C.   maintain the nerve membrane in a state of depolarization
    D.   prevent increased permeability of the nerve membrane to potassium ions
    E.   interfere with intracellular nerve metabolism

5.   Which of the following statements MOST accurately describes the effectiveness of action   5.____
of methyldopa? It

    A.   causes marked cardiac slowing
    B.   directly relaxes vascular smooth muscle
    C.   causes rapid depletion of norepinephrine from adrenergic nerve terminals
    D.   causes formation of a false transmitter which is released at vascular smooth mus-
cle
    E.   produces a false transmitter, the effect of which is primarily at central nuclei

6.   Which of the following effects of nitroglycerin are antagonized by propranolol?   6.____

    A.   Increase in heart rate
    B.   Relaxation of arterial smooth muscle

C. Relaxation of nonvascular smooth muscle
D. Decrease in left ventricular end diastolic pressure
E. None of the above

7. Which of the following drugs is BEST to administer after poisoning by an organophos-   7.___
phate cholinesterase inhibitor?

A. Atropine   B. Phenytoin
C. Pralidoxime   D. Propantheline
E. Phenobarbital

8. Which of the following statements is TRUE regarding streptomycin? It   8.___

A. is bactericidal
B. has a gram-positive spectrum
C. is usually administered orally
D. disrupts bacterial cell membranes
E. is associated with a low incidence of bacterial resistance

9. Which of the following drugs chelates with calcium?   9.___

A. Erythromycin   B. Polymyxin B
C. Tetracycline   D. Penicillin G
E. Chloramphenicol

10. Which of the following has the GREATEST sodium-retaining effect in comparison with   10.___
cortisone?

A. Prednisone   B. Aldosterone
C. Prednisolone   D. Triamcinolone
E. Dexamethasone

11. Morphine and its surrogates produce their MAJOR effects by activating the receptors for   11.___

A. prostaglandin   B. histamine
C. bradykinin   D. enkephalin
E. 5-hydroxytryptamine

12. Which of the following plasma proteins has the GREATEST ability to bind drugs?   12.___

A. Albumin   B. Fibrinogen
C. Hemoglobin   D. Gamma globulin
E. Beta lipoprotein

13. Which of the following antibiotics is the substitute of choice for penicillin in the penicillin-   13.___
sensitive patient?

A. Bacitracin   B. Erythromycin
C. Tetracycline   D. Chloramphenicol
E. Enderin

14. Which of the following prescriptions CANNOT be repeated without written authority?   14.___

A. ASA, 300 mg.
B. Chloral hydrate, 500 mg.
C. Codeine phosphate, 30 mg.
D. Diazepam, 10 mg.
E. ASA, 300 mg., with caffeine, 30 mg., and codeine, 30 mg.

15. Which of the following drugs is NOT used as an analgesic?   15._____

    A. Morphine   B. Nalorphine
    C. Meperidine   D. Levorphanol
    E. Alphaprodine

16. Which of the following is NOT a property of diphenhy-dramine? It   16._____

    A. relieves bronchospasm induced by histamine
    B. blocks the depressor effect of isoproterenol
    C. inhibits wheal formation after intracutaneous histamine
    D. inhibits contractions of isolated intestine caused by histamine
    E. reduces anaphylaxis induced by horse serum in sensitized guinea pigs

17. Which of the following is NOT true regarding coumarin anticoagulants?   17._____

    A. Administered orally
    B. Slow onset of action
    C. Antimetabolites of vitamin K
    D. Highly bound to plasma proteins
    E. Differ in their mechanisms of action

18. Which of the following is NOT true regarding acetaminophen? It   18._____

    A. has antipyretic properties
    B. may induce methemoglobinemia
    C. can be combined with codeine
    D. has anti-inflammatory properties
    E. is not cross-allergenic with aspirin

19. Which of the following statements does NOT characterize pentazocine?   19._____

    A. It is equianalgesic with codeine.
    B. It is a partial opioid antagonist.
    C. Its abuse potential is less than that of heroin.
    D. It may induce dysphoria and mental aberrations.
    E. It is effective only on parenteral administration.

20. Which of the following statements is NOT true regarding barbiturates? They   20._____

    A. possess significant analgesic properties
    B. possess serious drug dependence potential
    C. vary in degree of lipid solubility
    D. possess anticonvulsant properties
    E. suppress REM sleep

21. Epinephrine, when administered intravenously in high dose, would NOT be expected to   21._____

    A. increase liver glycogenolysis
    B. cause bronchiolar constriction
    C. produce a rise in blood pressure
    D. evoke extrasystoles in the heart
    E. produce restlessness and anxiety

22. A local anesthetic injected into an inflamed area will NOT give maximum effects because   22.___
    A. the pH of inflamed tissue inhibits the release of the free base
    B. the drug will not be absorbed as rapidly because of the decreased blood supply
    C. the chemical mediators of inflammation will present a chemical antagonism to the anesthetic
    D. prostaglandins stabilize the nerve membrane and diminish the effectiveness of the local anesthetic
    E. of local shock

23. Each of the following drugs can be used in the prevention or treatment of angina pectoris   23.___
    EXCEPT
    A. digitalis
    B. propranolol
    C. nitroglycerin
    D. isosorbide dinitrate
    E. pentaerythritol tetranitrate

24. All of the following drugs are useful in the treatment of hypertension EXCEPT   24.___
    A. ephedrine   B. reserpine
    C. methyldopa   D. thiazide diuretics
    E. none of the above

25. All of the following agents are metabolized mainly by hydrolysis of the ester linkage   25.___
    EXCEPT
    A. procaine   B. lidocaine
    C. piperocaine   D. chloroprocaine
    E. metabutethamine

KEY (CORRECT ANSWERS)

1.	D	11.	D
2.	E	12.	A
3.	B	13.	B
4.	B	14.	C
5.	E	15.	B
6.	A	16.	B
7.	C	17.	E
8.	A	18.	D
9.	C	19.	E
10.	B	20.	A

21.	B
22.	A
23.	A
24.	A
25.	B

———————

TEST 2

DIRECTIONS: Each question or incomplete statement is followed by several suggested answers or completions. Select the one that BEST answers the question or completes the statement. *PRINT THE LETTER OF THE CORRECT ANSWER IN THE SPACE AT THE RIGHT.*

1. The central actions of ethyl alcohol are synergistic with all of the following EXCEPT   1.__

   A. caffeine   B. diazepam
   C. meperidine   D. barbiturates
   E. phenothiazines

2. All of the following are contraindications to the use of oral contraceptives EXCEPT   2.__

   A. hyperthyroidism
   B. hypertension
   C. history of breast cancer
   D. undiagnosed genital bleeding
   E. history of thromboembolic disease

3. All of the following statements are TRUE regarding ethyl alcohol EXCEPT that   3.__

   A. it has diuretic properties
   B. it initially stimulates the CNS
   C. it dilates blood vessels of the skin
   D. its emetic effects are due to local gastric as well as central effects
   E. blood levels in excess of 500 mg. % usually result in coma and death

4. All of the following influence the rate of induction during anesthesia EXCEPT   4.__

   A. pulmonary ventilation
   B. blood supply to the lungs
   C. hemoglobin content of the blood
   D. concentration of the anesthetic in the inspired mixture
   E. solubility of the anesthetic in blood (blood-gas partition coefficient, Ostwald coefficient)

5. Each of the following drugs is considered to be a direct-acting catecholamine EXCEPT   5.__

   A. epinephrine   B. amphetamine
   C. isoproterenol   D. norepinephrine
   E. none of the above

6. All of the following pertain to general anesthesia induced by thiopental EXCEPT   6.__

   A. fast induction   B. decreased secretions
   C. low therapeutic index   D. short duration of anesthesia
   E. predisposition to laryngospasm

7. All of the following factors are significant determinants of the duration of conduction block with amide-type local anesthetics EXCEPT the   7.__

   A. pH of tissues in the area of injection
   B. degree of vasodilatation caused by the local anesthetic

    C. blood plasma cholinesterase levels
    D. blood flow through the area of conduction block
    E. concentration of the injected anesthetic solution

8. All of the following are TRUE regarding the intravenous agent ketamine EXCEPT that it   8.____

    A. produces hypnosis and true anesthesia
    B. produces "dissociative anesthesia"
    C. may produce tonic and clonic convulsions
    D. is now used primarily in children
    E. may produce delirium, hallucinations and schizoid reactions

9. Symptoms of digitalis toxicity include all of the following EXCEPT   9.____

    A. extrasystoles   B. nausea and vomiting
    C. yellow-green vision   D. A-V conduction block
    E. decreased P-R interval

10. Each of the following drugs is used in the management of epilepsy EXCEPT   10.____

    A. phenytoin   B. ethosuximide
    C. valproic acid   D. phenobarbital
    E. diphenhydramine

11. All of the following statements are TRUE regarding the general aspects of toxicology   11.____
EXCEPT that

    A. most drugs exert a single action
    B. toxicity is both time- and dose-dependent
    C. toxicity can be due to overdosage of a drug
    D. toxicity can be anything ranging from nausea to death
    E. for some drugs, even very minimal concentrations can be harmful

12. Central skeletal muscle relaxation produced by depression of the polysynaptic reflex arcs   12.____
is brought about by all of the following drugs EXCEPT

    A. diazepam   B. meprobamate
    C. lorazepam   D. tubocurarine
    E. none of the above

13. Advantages of inhalation sedation with nitrous oxide include all of the following EXCEPT   13.____

    A. short recovery time
    B. rapid onset of action
    C. rapid biotransformation in the liver
    D. ability to alter the depth of sedation from moment to moment
    E. none of the above

14. All of the following statements are TRUE about anti-neoplastic agents EXCEPT that   14.____

    A. generally they are not curative, although the success rate is improving
    B. most agents possess a very high therapeutic index
    C. generally they do not possess a selective effect on neoplastic cells
    D. they are most effective in widely disseminated, non-solid tumors
    E. they tend to suppress function of the bone marrow

15. All of the following are pharmacologic and toxicologic properties of aspirin EXCEPT   15.___

    A. tinnitus
    B. analgesia
    C. salicylism
    D. antipyresis
    E. suppression of the immune response

16. All of the following statements with regard to the auto-coid prostaglandin are correct   16.___
EXCEPT that

    A. it is a fatty acid
    B. it is derived from essential amino acids
    C. it is thought to be involved in the inflammatory process
    D. it is thought to be involved in the reproductive process
    E. its synthesis may be inhibited by nonsteroidal, anti-inflammatory agents

17. All of the following are examples of iatrogenic diseases EXCEPT   17.___

    A. development of peptic ulcer with chronic use of aspirin
    B. development of gout with use of thiazide diuretics
    C. blood dyscrasias with use of chloramphenicol
    D. pseudomembranous colitis from use of clindamycin
    E. increased potassium excretion from hyperaldosteronism

18. Vasoconstricting drugs are included in local anesthetic solutions for all of the following   18.___
reasons EXCEPT to

    A. reduce the toxicity of local anesthetics
    B. prolong the duration of action of local anesthetics
    C. reduce the rate of vascular absorption of local anesthetics
    D. increase the concentration of the local anesthetic at the nerve membrane
    E. prevent penetration of the local anesthetic at the nerve membrane

19. All of the following statements are TRUE regarding intra-venous diazepam EXCEPT that   19.___
it

    A. has a low therapeutic index
    B. produces some degree of amnesia
    C. can be employed to terminate most convulsive states
    D. is locally irritating to tissue and may produce local thrombophlebitis
    E. does not cause significant cardiovascular and respiratory depressions with normal
       use

20. Hydrocortisone may be expected to be effective in each of the following conditions   20.___
EXCEPT

    A. allergic urticaria
    B. temporomandibular arthritis
    C. ulcerative oral lesions
    D. penicillin anaphylaxis
    E. acute adrenocortical insufficiency

21. All of the following symptoms are associated with neostigmine poisoning EXCEPT   21.____

    A. diarrhea   B. salivation
    C. convulsions   D. bronchiolar constriction
    E. skeletal muscle paralysis

22. Heparin has all of the following effects EXCEPT   22.____

    A. activation of plasma antithrombin
    B. blocking of thromboplastin generation
    C. neutralization of tissue thromboplastin
    D. reduction of circulating fibrinogen
    E. clearing of alimentary hyperlipemia

23. Xerostomia is a common side effect of all of the following EXCEPT   23.____

    A. clonidine   B. reserpine
    C. imipramine   D. scopolamine
    E. promethazine

24. Which of the following diuretics is appropriate for a patient who is suffering from conges-   24.____
tive heart failure and tends to show digitalis toxicity?

    A. Furosemide   B. Triamterene
    C. Ethacrynic acid   D. Trichlormethiazide
    E. Hydrochlorothiazide

25. Which of the following antibiotics is LEAST likely to cause superinfection?   25.____

    A. Gentamicin   B. Tetracycline
    C. Penicillin G   D. Streptomycin
    E. Chloramphenicol

KEY (CORRECT ANSWERS)

1.	A		11.	A
2.	A		12.	D
3.	B		13.	C
4.	C		14.	B
5.	B		15.	E
6.	B		16.	B
7.	C		17.	E
8.	A		18.	E
9.	E		19.	A
10.	E		20.	D

21.	C
22.	D
23.	B
24.	B
25.	C

EXAMINATION SECTION
TEST 1

DIRECTIONS: Each question or incomplete statement is followed by several suggested answers or completions. Select the one that BEST answers the question or completes the statement. *PRINT THE LETTER OF THE CORRECT ANSWER IN THE SPACE AT THE RIGHT.*

1. Research indicates that among the following psychological factors, the one most likely to increase an individual's potential for substance dependence is a(n)

    A.   internal locus of control
    B.   *Type A* personality
    C.   high feeling of self-worth
    D.   tendency toward risk-seeking behavior

1.____

2. Of the following substances, the use of_____ is most clearly linked to violent crime.

    A.   marijuana
    B.   alcohol
    C.   LSD
    D.   heroin

2.____

3. The neurotransmitter that is inhibited by sedative hypnotics is

    A.   GABA
    B.   dopamine
    C.   acetylcholine
    D.   serotonin

3.____

4. At moderate doses, stimulants can produce

    A.   paranoia
    B.   a sense of well-being
    C.   a dreamy/sleepy state
    D.   a loss of inhibitions

4.____

5. *Chipping* is a term that refers to the attempt to distribute lower doses of_____ at intervals that will avoid addiction.

    A.   heroin
    B.   marijuana
    C.   cocaine
    D.   alcohol

5.____

6. Amphetamines

    A.   can cause panic, agitation, hallucinations, and paranoid delusions
    B.   generally increase appetite and decrease fatigue
    C.   block the reception of dopamine in the nervous system
    D.   cause a period of depression and fatigue that is usually followed by feelings of euphoria

6.____

7. A person who is designated as a *Type 2* alcoholic has   7.____

     A. comorbid diabetes
     B. developed the disease early in life
     C. limited mobility
     D. a pronounced serotonin deficit in the brain

8. A common model of substance abuse has the person beginning with beer, wine, or ciga-   8.____
rettes, and then moving on to hard liquor and marijuana, and subsequently to other illicit
drugs. This progression is known as

     A. the tolerance curve
     B. situational use
     C. staging
     D. compulsion

9. The most appropriate goal of drug education programs is to   9.____

     A. relay information
     B. screen for likely drug users
     C. modify pre-addictive behaviors
     D. gather information from attendants

10. The primary factor in the decline in alcohol use among high school students from 1980 to   10.____
the first decade of the 21st century was

     A. a trickle-down effect from the decline in alcohol use among college students
     B. a decline in binge drinking
     C. an increase in the use of illicit drugs
     D. less accessibility to alcohol

11. The most widely prescribed class of drugs in the United States is   11.____

     A. steroids
     B. barbiturates
     C. opiates
     D. benzodiazepines

12. The most likely cause of death among heavy users of alcohol is   ' 12.____

     A. cardiovascular disease
     B. cirrhosis of the liver
     C. digestive disorders
     D. vehicular accidents

13. Cocaethylene, a dangerous drug metabolite, is produced by the combination of cocaine   13.____
and

     A. alcohol
     B. heroin
     C. marijuana
     D. LSD

14. _____ is a central nervous system depressant.   14._____

    A. Heroin
    B. Marijuana
    C. Cocaine
    D. Alcohol

15. The main reason for the lengthy amount of time it takes to metabolize and excrete mari-   15._____
juana is that it is

    A. excreted only by the lungs
    B. stored in fat cells for up to several weeks after each use
    C. an inhaled particulate, rather than a liquid or solid
    D. one of the main components in renal calculi (kidney stones)

16. Among problem drinkers, the personality characteristic that is MOST likely to be shared   16._____
is

    A. personal maladjustment
    B. depression
    C. emotional immaturity
    D. sexual dysfunction or deviance

17. Which of the following is a prominent SSRI (selective serotonin reuptake inhibitor) drug?   17._____

    A. Miltown
    B. Valium
    C. Darvon
    D. Prozac

18. Alcohol begins to influence the brain, vision, and decision-making at a blood alcohol con-   18._____
centration (BAC) of about

    A. 0.01
    B. 0.02
    C. 0.04
    D. 0.08

19. _____ is a term that refers to the violent behavior that results from the conflict inherent   19._____
in the drug trade.

    A. Transferred intent
    B. Global wave
    C. Systemic link
    D. Collateral damage

20. The_____ theory of substance dependence holds that eventually, the vicious cycle   20._____
develops in which the motivation for drug taking shifts from a desire for the euphoric high
to the need to relive an increasingly intense *down* feeling that follows drug use.

    A. moral weakness
    B. circular reasoning
    C. gateway
    D. opponent-process

21. When compared to other routes of administration, drugs administered _____ are gen-   21.____
    erally absorbed more slowly.

    A. by intravenous injection
    B. by intramuscular injection
    C. orally
    D. by inhalation

22. The substance_____ is used to treat overdose from heroin and other opioids by block-   22.____
    ing the receptors that normally bind with the drug.

    A. naloxone
    B. clonidine
    C. disulfiram
    D. methadone

23. The antipsychotic drug chlorpromazine (Thorazine) is sometimes used to block the   23.____
    effects of each of the following, EXCEPT

    A. psilocybin
    B. mescaline
    C. PCP
    D. LSD

24. The neurotransmitter_____ is a primary agent in the *pleasure pathway* in the brain,   24.____
    which is believed to be involved in substance dependence.

    A. dopamine
    B. norepinephrine
    C. serotonin
    D. acetylcholine

25. Alcohol withdrawal symptoms can include   25.____
    I. convulsions
    II. insomnia
    III. tremors
    IV. hallucinations

    A. I, II and III
    B. II only
    C. II and III
    D. I, II, III and IV

KEY (CORRECT ANSWERS)

1.	D	11.	D
2.	B	12.	D
3.	A	13.	A
4.	A	14.	D
5.	A	15.	B
6.	A	16.	A
7.	B	17.	D
8.	C	18.	B
9.	A	19.	C
10.	D	20.	D

21.	C
22.	A
23.	C
24.	A
25.	D

TEST 2

DIRECTIONS: Each question or incomplete statement is followed by several suggested answers or completions. Select the one that BEST answers the question or completes the statement. *PRINT THE LETTER OF THE CORRECT ANSWER IN THE SPACE AT THE RIGHT.*

1. The medical approach to alcoholism, which views it as a disease, also holds that the only acceptable goal is   1.____

    A. a lifetime prescription of Antabuse
    B. total abstinence
    C. controlled social drinking with trusted friends and family members
    D. inpatient confinement

2. Which of the following is NOT a typical symptom of alcohol withdrawal?   2.____

    A. Sweating
    B. Irritability
    C. Flushed skin
    D. Depression

3. In the human brain, a respiratory center necessary for breathing is located in the   3.____

    A. hindbrain
    B. cerebellum
    C. medulla
    D. thalamus

4. _____ prevention programs are designed to prevent substance dependence before it begins.   4.____

    A. Primary
    B. Secondary
    C. Tertiary
    D. Quaternary

5. Which of the following is NOT a synthetic opiate?   5.____

    A. Fentanyl
    B. Morphine
    C. Methadone
    D. Meperidine

6. Benzodiazepines are prescribed primarily to treat   6.____

    A. substance dependence
    B. depression
    C. anxiety
    D. pain

7. The area of the brain most effected by tetrahydrocannabinol (THC) is the   7.____

    A. hippocampus
    B. hypothalamus
    C. cerebrum
    D. medulla

8. The primary feature of substance abuse is the 8.____

    A. usage of increasing amounts to achieve the same high
    B. feeling of a need for the substance
    C. use of the substance in order to prevent withdrawal
    D. continued use of a substance de spite risks or problems in living

9. Currently, methaqualone is a Schedule _____ drug. 9.____

    A. I
    B. II
    C. III
    D. IV

10. Among the elderly, the most common trigger event for excessive drinking is 10.____

    A. crime victimization
    B. retirement
    C. the death of a spouse
    D. the death of a child

11. Which of the following is a benzodiazepine? 11.____

    A. Placidyl
    B. Nembutal
    C. Valium
    D. Miltown

12. Clinically, opioids 12.____

    A. stimulate awareness
    B. have no medically recognized use
    C. increase appetite
    D. relieve pain

13. Alcoholic dementia is associated with 13.____

    A. an enlargement of the brain ventricles
    B. liver damage
    C. a permanent reduction in acetylcholine receptors
    D. a damaged hypothalamus

14. Which of the following factors is LEAST likely to result in a decrease in the intoxicating 14.____
effect of a drug?

    A. concurrent intake of food
    B. increase in body fat stores
    C. greater body mass
    D. fewer body fat stores

15. Generally, the most dangerous combination of substances occurs with   15.___

    A. alcohol and marijuana
    B. alcohol and sedative hypnotics
    C. hallucinogens and narcotics
    D. amphetamines and sedative hypnotics

16. Which of the following is a risk factor for alcoholism?   16.___

    A. Not completing high school
    B. Being male
    C. Being African-American
    D. Being married

17. The route of administration that puts a drug into the layer of fat directly beneath the skin   17.___
is

    A. inunction
    B. transdermal injection
    C. intramuscular injection
    D. subcutaneous injection

18. Which of the following is NOT an immediate effect of nitrous oxide?   18.___

    A. Euphoria
    B. Dehydration
    C. Cardiac arrhythmia
    D. Spontaneous laughter

19. LSD research has demonstrated that   19.___

    A. it is physiologically addictive
    B. tolerance is acquired rapidly
    C. it is absorbed slowly through the GI tract
    D. it is taken up selectively by the brain

20. In adulthood, the factor that is most closely linked to the onset of alcoholism is   20.___

    A. peer relations
    B. ethnic identity
    C. family history of alcoholism
    D. socioeconomic status

21. A primary duty of the federal Drug Enforcement Agency (DEA) is to   21.___

    A. enforce federal laws related to illicit narcotic drugs and cooperating with state and
        local agencies in the enforcement of state narcotics laws
    B. conduct drug abuse prevention programs
    C. gather intelligence on traffickers in illicit drugs
    D. regulate the flow and manufacture of legal but controlled drugs

22. At moderate doses, opiates can produce

22.____

    A. hypertension
    B. hypothermia
    C. respiratory depression
    D. constricted pupils

23. For most alcoholics, the first step in treatment is

23.____

    A. the first of the Twelve Steps
    B. detoxification
    C. individual therapy
    D. inpatient admission

24. *Club drugs* often used by young adults at all-night dance parties or at dance clubs and bars, include each of the following, EXCEPT

24.____

    A. ketamine
    B. GHB (gamma hydroxybutyrate)
    C. marijuana
    D. MDMA (ecstasy)

25. The most widely used opiate antagonist in withdrawal treatment is

25.____

    A. methadone
    B. clonidine
    C. chlorpromazine
    D. naltrexone

KEY (CORRECT ANSWERS)

1. B		11. C	
2. C		12. D	
3. C		13. A	
4. A		14. D	
5. B		15. B	
6. C		16. B	
7. A		17. D	
8. D		18. B	
9. A		19. B	
10. C		20. C	

21.	D
22.	B
23.	B
24.	C
25.	D

TEST 3

DIRECTIONS: Each question or incomplete statement is followed by several suggested answers or completions. Select the one that BEST answers the question or completes the statement. *PRINT THE LETTER OF THE CORRECT ANSWER IN THE SPACE AT THE RIGHT.*

1. Which of the following sedative hypnotics is neither a barbiturate nor a benzodiazepine?　　1.___

   A. Methaqualone
   B. Chlorazepate
   C. Diazepam
   D. Secobarbital

2. A substance that effectively increases the activity of a neurotransmitter by binding with a cell receptor and causing a response is known as a(n)　　2.___

   A. barbiturate
   B. narcotic
   C. agonist
   D. analgesic

3. Which of the following is an opioid, developed for pharmaceutical use in the 1990s, which has proven to be addictive for many users?　　3.___

   A. OxyContin
   B. Fen-Phen
   C. Tamgesic
   D. St. John's wort

4. Which of the following routes of administration greatly increases a drug user's risk for hepatitis and AIDS?　　4.___

   A. Inhalation
   B. Ingestion (oral)
   C. Parenteral (injection)
   D. Topical (absorption through the skin)

5. The form of cannabis with the weakest concentration of tetrahydrocan-nabinol (THC) is　　5.___

   A. marijuana
   B. sinsemilla
   C. hashish
   D. hashish oil

6. Each year, about 75 percent of the drug-related deaths in the United States are associated with　　6.___

   A. alcohol
   B. polydrug episodes
   C. narcotics
   D. cocaine

7. The drug most often abused by adolescents is marijuana, followed by   7.____

    A. cocaine
    B. MDMA (ecstasy)
    C. barbiturates
    D. inhalants

8. What is the term for the interaction that takes place when two drugs are mixed together   8.____
   to produce a greater effect than that of either drug taken separately?

    A. Antagonism
    B. Potentiation
    C. Pronunciation
    D. Agonism

9. The oxidative rate-the rate at which the body metabolizes a substance-for alcohol in   9.____
   adults is a little under

    A. one drink per hour
    B. two drinks per hour
    C. three drinks in two hours
    D. four drinks per day

10. Which of the following is a common side effect associated with the use of antidepressant   10.____
    drugs, especially tricyclics (Elavil) and Serotonin and norepinephrine reuptake inhibitors
    (SNRIs)?

    A. Sweating
    B. Blotchy skin
    C. Constipation
    D. Ruid retention

11. _____ programs are designed to minimize the physiological changes associated with   11.____
    withdrawal from a substance.

    A. Withdrawal
    B. Therapeutic community
    C. 12-step
    D. Milieu

12. The most widely used sedative hypnotic drug is   12.____

    A. Seconal
    B. alcohol
    C. diazepam
    D. methaqualone

13. Of all Americans who complete a drug treatment program, the percentage who remain   13.____
    drug-free for at least a year afterward is about

    A. 5-10
    B. 15-35
    C. 30-50
    D. 60-80

14. *Speedball* is a street term that refers to the combination of   14.____

    A. methamphetamine and heroin
    B. cocaine and heroin
    C. cocaine and methamphetamine
    D. methamphetamine and LSD

15. Neurotransmitters are synthesized and metabolized in the body by   15.____

    A. enzymes
    B. amino acids
    C. axons
    D. metabolites

16. A substance that produces vivid sensory awareness or feelings of increased insight is   16.____
    said to have_____ properties.

    A. hallucinogenic
    B. psychedelic
    C. barbiturate
    D. narcotic

17. Which of the following is NOT a fundamental process associated with the concept of   17.____
    addiction?

    A. Reinforcement
    B. Tolerance
    C. Physical dependence
    D. Affective disorder

18. Blood alcohol concentration (BAC) becomes lethal at about   18.____

    A. 0.2
    B. 0.4
    C. 0.8
    D. 1.0

19. Which of the following is a common side effect of antipsychotic drugs?   19.____

    A. Photosensitivity
    B. Excitability
    C. Alzheimer's disease
    D. Constipation

20. Nembutal and Seconal are   20.____

    A. opiates
    B. barbiturates
    C. benzodiazepines
    D. stimulants

21. Of the following, the substance that causes the greatest overall damage to human tissue is

    A. marijuana
    B. LSD
    C. cocaine
    D. alcohol

21._____

22. Which of the following is NOT used as an alternative to anabolic steroids?

    A. Clonidine
    B. Clenbuterol
    C. GHB (gamma hydroxybutyrate)
    D. Androstenedione

22._____

23. The most likely result of drinking excessively before bedtime in order to relax is_____, which may produce anxiety and restlessness.

    A. nightmares
    B. hypertension
    C. dream deficit
    D. sleep deficit

23._____

24. Which of the following was originally used as a nasal decongestant?

    A. Cocaine
    B. Amphetamine
    C. Opium
    D. Morphine

24._____

25. The phenomenon that most clearly demonstrates that there is a cognitive as well as physiological factor involved in drug reaction and dependence is the

    A. disease model
    B. opponent-process theory
    C. expectancy effect
    D. contingency management

25._____

KEY (CORRECT ANSWERS)

1.	A		11.	A
2.	C		12.	B
3.	A		13.	C
4.	C		14.	B
5.	A		15.	A
6.	B		16.	A
7.	D		17.	D
8.	B		18.	B
9.	A		19.	A
10.	C		20.	B

21. D
22. A
23. C
24. B
25. C

———

TEST 4

DIRECTIONS: Each question or incomplete statement is followed by several suggested answers or completions. Select the one that BEST answers the question or completes the statement. *PRINT THE LETTER OF THE CORRECT ANSWER IN THE SPACE AT THE RIGHT.*

1. The *amotivational syndrome* is a controversial theory that refers to an indifference to long-range plans among habitual users of

    A. alcohol
    B. cocaine
    C. heroin
    D. marijuana

1.____

2. Which of the following hallucinogens is derived from the peyote cactus?

    A. Mescaline
    B. Psilocybin
    C. Atropine
    D. Harmaline

2.____

3. Which of the following is NOT an effect associated with the use of anabolic steroids in men?

    A. Increased sex drive
    B. Gynecomastia (breast development)
    C. Hair loss
    D. Increased blood cholesterol

3.____

4. The most extensively used illicit drug in the United States today is

    A. marijuana
    B. amphetamine
    C. cocaine
    D. anabolic steroids

4.____

5. The primary area of the brain that is inhibited by alcohol intoxication is the

    A. hippocampus
    B. medulla
    C. cerebrum
    D. hypothalamus

5.____

6. Generally, the most difficult time in the process of withdrawal from heroin addiction occurs from_____ hours after the last use.

    A. 6 to 12
    B. 12 to 24
    C. 24 to 72
    D. 72 to 96

6.____

7. Physical dependence on a drug is most closely associated with   7.____

    A. escalating use
    B. withdrawal symptoms
    C. missing days of work or school
    D. a strong compulsion to use the drug

8. Which of the following neurotransmitters is released at the somatic neuromuscular junc-   8.____
tions?

    A. Dopamine
    B. Epinephrine
    C. Acetylcholine
    D. Serotonin

9. Alcohol's most significant health-related impact occurs in the_____ system.   9.____

    A. respiratory
    B. digestive
    C. endocrine
    D. central nervous

10. An effect common to the use of most inhalants is   10.____

    A. spontaneous laughter
    B. dizziness
    C. headache
    D. a loss of inhibition

11. Compared to cocaine, the stimulating effects of amphetamines are   11.____

    A. about the same in duration and intensity
    B. longer-lasting and more intense
    C. shorter-lasting and more intense
    D. longer-lasting and less intense

12. Drugs that are classified as *psychedelics* because they enhancing perceptive and   12.____
thought processes of the brain include each of the following, EXCEPT

    A. LSD
    B. psilocybin
    C. mescaline
    D. ketamine

13. A disorder common among alcoholics, caused by vitamin B_1 deficiency and character-   13.____
ized by disorientation, confusion, abnormal eye movements, and amnesia, is_____ syndrome

    A. Ackerman's
    B. Korsakoff's
    C. Tourette's
    D. Reye's

14. The use of which of the following drugs is MOST likely to lead to tolerance or physical   14.____
    dependence?

    A. PCP (phencyclidine)
    B. Marijuana
    C. Amphetamine
    D. LSD

15. Common symptoms of cocaine abuse include each of the following, EXCEPT   15.____

    A. insomnia
    B. runny nose
    C. constricted pupils
    D. talkativeness

16. Available statistics on drugs and crime in the United States suggest that most narcotic   16.____
    addicts who commit crimes

    A. commit mostly *victimless* crimes
    B. are under the influence when they commit crimes
    C. began criminal activity after they became addicted
    D. were engaged in criminal activity before they became addicted

17. Most drugs and metabolites are excreted   17.____

    A. in the form of perspiration, saliva, and tears
    B. in the form of air expired by the lungs
    C. by the gallbladder
    D. by the kidneys

18. Which of the following drugs is used to reduce the severity of narcotic withdrawal symp-   18.____
    toms?

    A. Clonidine
    B. Fentanyl
    C. Naltrexone
    D. Hydrocodone

19. Each of the following is a risk factor for alcohol abuse, EXCEPT   19.____

    A. peer relations
    B. a high tolerance for alcohol
    C. family relations
    D. heredity

20. By using alcohol, a person can induce an increased tolerance for Seconal, despite the   20.____
    fact that the user has never taken Seconal before. This is an example of

    A. distributive effect
    B. a breach in the blood-brain barrier
    C. cross-tolerance
    D. agonism

21. The class of drugs to which Ritalin belongs, and which are now the drugs of choice for treating attention-deficit/hyperactivity disorder, are

    A. stimulants
    B. depressants
    C. narcotics
    D. sedative hypnotics

21.____

22. Of the following substances, which is a narcotic?

    A. Heroin
    B. Amphetamine
    C. Alcohol
    D. LSD

22.____

23. Dexedrine and Benzedrine are commonly abused

    A. benzodiazepines
    B. amphetamines
    C. narcotics
    D. barbiturates

23.____

24. Nationwide, the primary purpose of the Drug Abuse Warning Network (DAWN) is to

    A. monitor drug-related hospital emergency department (ED) visits and drug-related deaths
    B. establish in-school programs that teach children about the consequences of drug abuse
    C. establish a network of drug treatment centers
    D. monitor the international trade in illicit drugs

24.____

25. The third stage of alcoholism, in which there is a loss of control of drinking and occasional binges of heavy drinking, is the_____ stage.

    A. pre-alcoholic
    B. chronic
    C. prodromal
    D. crucial

25.____

KEY (CORRECT ANSWERS)

1.	D		11.	D
2.	A		12.	D
3.	A		13.	B
4.	A		14.	C
5.	C		15.	C
6.	C		16.	D
7.	B		17.	D
8.	C		18.	A
9.	D		19.	B
10.	D		20.	C

21.	A
22.	A
23.	B
24.	A
25.	D

EXAMINATION SECTION
TEST 1

DIRECTIONS: Each question or incomplete statement is followed by several suggested answers or completions. Select the one that BEST answers the question or completes the statement. *PRINT THE LETTER OF THE CORRECT ANSWER IN THE SPACE AT THE RIGHT.*

1. Research indicates that among all users of illicit drugs in the United States, about _____ percent use marijuana.

   A. 35   B. 50
   C. 65   D. 80

   1.____

2. A drug's "anxiolytic" effect refers to its ability to

   A. relieve pain   B. relieve anxiety
   C. metabolize rapidly   D. produce a euphoric feeling

   2.____

3. The mandrake and datura plants contain each of the following hallucinogens, EXCEPT

   A. scopolamine   B. mescaline
   C. hyoscyamine   D. atropine

   3.____

4. A drug dependence that results from a physician's treatment for a recognized medical condition is known as _____ addiction.

   A. nosocomial   B. incidental
   C. iatrogenic   D. clinical

   4.____

5. The subjective effects of barbiturates are practically indistinguishable from those of

   A. amphetamine   B. alcohol
   C. hallucinogens   D. benzodiazepines

   5.____

6. Home drug testing kits are typically sensitive to evidence of each of the following, EXCEPT

   A. LSD   B. alcohol
   C. amphetamine   D. cocaine

   6.____

7. The major portion of an alcoholic drink is metabolized by the

   A. liver   B. stomach
   C. pancreas   D. brain

   7.____

8. The family and friends of a person suffering from substance dependence decide to stage an intervention. Which of the following is generally believed to be a component in an effective intervention?

   A. Convincing the substance abuser that dependence is a problem that is easily overcome.
   B. Making a specific list of the substance abuser's transgressions over the past several months.
   C. Focusing on all the ways in which the substance abuser is still able to function in family and society, despite his or her dependence.
   D. Emphasizing care and concern for the substance abuser.

   8.____

9. Approximately what percentage of the antidepressants prescribed in the United States today are prescribed by physicians who are not psychiatrists?

   A. 10   B. 33
   C. 50   D. 75

9._____

10. Among older teenagers and young adults, one of the most powerful and consistent predictors for drug abuse is

   A. school problems   B. personal/family crisis
   C. failed or failing relationships   D. peer pressure

10._____

11. The greatest amount of direct societal costs, in terms of the "behavioral toxicity" of a substance, is associated in the United States with the abuse of

   A. cocaine   B. marijuana
   C. heroin   D. alcohol

11._____

12. Which of the following is NOT one of the classic signs of opiate overdose?

   A. Constricted pupils   B. Coma
   C. Nausea   D. Respiratory depression

12._____

13. The rate at which alcohol is absorbed into the bloodstream is affected by each of the following, EXCEPT the

   A. person's metabolic rate
   B. mixing of a drink with a carbonated beverage
   C. alcoholic concentration of the beverage
   D. time of day the drink is consumed

13._____

14. The rate of drug absorption is greatest in the

   A. large intestine   B. small intestine
   C. stomach   D. liver

14._____

15. In the human nervous system, information is transmitted outward from the nerve cell body by the

   A. mitochondrion   B. synapse
   C. dendrite   D. axon

15._____

16. Which of the following is NOT typically used as a "date rape" drug?

   A. Rohypnol   B. Ketamine
   C. Ecstasy (MDMA)   D. GHB (gamma hydroxybutyrate)

16._____

17. Which of the following is a street term for a smokeable form of amphetamine?

   A. Eight-ball   B. Smack
   C. Ice   D. Rock

17._____

18. The highest rate of adolescent drug use is found in

   A. the United States   B. Thailand
   C. Russia   D. France

18._____

19. Which of the following is a naturally occurring chemical in the brain hat has an effect similar to THC?

    A. Enkephalin   B. Disulfiram
    C. GABA   D. Anandamide

19.____

20. Which of the following is a synthetic opiate that is used to treat heroin withdrawal by satisfying cravings?

    A. Naloxone   B. Morphine
    C. Methadone   D. Disulfiram

20.____

21. Which of the following is an inhibitory neurotransmitter?

    A. GABA   B. Serotonin
    C. Acetylcholine   D. Norepinephrine

21.____

22. Death due to accidental overdose is MOST likely to be associated with the use of

    A. LSD   B. stimulants
    C. barbiturates   D. alcohol

22.____

23. Common symptoms of marijuana use include each of the following, EXCEPT

    A. talkativeness   B. reddened eyes
    C. voracious appetite   D. slurred speech

23.____

24. Women tend to metabolize alcohol more slowly than men because they

    A. are generally smaller in size
    B. generally have a higher percentage of body fat
    C. tend to drink more slowly
    D. usually eat more while drinking

24.____

25. Disulfiram is used as a treatment for alcoholism. It acts by

    A. blocking the reception of alcohol by brain receptors
    B. immediately breaking down alcohol into its harmless component molecules
    C. producing an immediate and severe negative reaction to alcohol intake
    D. alleviating physical withdrawal symptoms

25.____

KEY (CORRECT ANSWERS)

1.	D		11.	D
2.	B		12.	C
3.	B		13.	D
4.	C		14.	B
5.	B		15.	D
6.	A		16.	C
7.	A		17.	C
8.	D		18.	A
9.	C		19.	D
10.	D		20.	C

21.	A
22.	C
23.	D
24.	B
25.	C

———

TEST 2

DIRECTIONS: Each question or incomplete statement is followed by several suggested answers or completions. Select the one that BEST answers the question or completes the statement. *PRINT THE LETTER OF THE CORRECT ANSWER IN THE SPACE AT THE RIGHT.*

1. The fastest growing cause of deaths related to illegal drug use today is

    A. alcohol/barbiturates overdose
    B. vehicular accidents among the intoxicated
    C. AIDS
    D. amphetamine overdose

    1._____

2. During the acute phase of a person's detoxification from substance dependence, the primary focus for those who are with him/her should be to

    A. monitor physiological withdrawal symptoms and vital signs
    B. monitor for emotional outbreaks
    C. maintain wariness against manipulative or deceptive behavior
    D. arrange rehabilitation counseling

    2._____

3. Among Americans, the highest rates of illicit drug use occur in the _____ age group.

    A. 11 to 18   B. 18 to 25
    C. 26 to 33   D. 34 to 41

    3._____

4. For most people, signs of intoxication such as staggering, slurring of speech, or belligerence are likely to appear after about _____ alcoholic drinks.

    A. 1 or 2   B. 3 or 4
    C. 5 or 6   D. 9 or 10

    4._____

5. The first federal Schedule of Controlled Substances was released in

    A. 1906   B. 1933
    C. 1970   D. 1984

    5._____

6. Which of the following is a hallucinogen that is chemically similar to acetylcholine?

    A. Atropine   B. Mescaline
    C. Psilocybin   D. LSD

    6._____

7. The "gateway theory" of drug use generally holds that a person's use of more dangerous illicit drugs is a predictable progression from his or her use of

    A. prescription opiates   B. marijuana
    C. inhalants   D. cocaine

    7._____

8. Which of the following drugs has NOT been associated with significant physical withdrawal symptoms in users?

    A. Alcohol   B. Caffeine
    C. LSD   D. Amphetamines

    8._____

9. Most drug screening programs are set up to test for

    A. the presence of drugs or metabolites in urine
    B. the presence of drugs or metabolites in blood

    9._____

    C.   altered brain wave activity
    D.   heart arrhythmias or other irregularities

10. Common symptoms of alcohol use include each of the following, EXCEPT   10.____

    A.   incoherent speech
    B.   bloodshot eyes
    C.   irregular walking or muscle movements
    D.   heightened perception

11. In the late 20th century, federal jurisdiction for the regulation of anabolic steroids was   11.____
    transferred from the

    A.   Drug Enforcement Agency (DEA) to the National Institutes of Health (NIH)
    B.   NIH to the DEA
    C.   Food and Drug Administration (FDA) to the DEA
    D.   U.S. Department of Agriculture (USDA) to the FDA

12. Delirium tremens is most likely to occur in the _____ phase of alcoholism.   12.____

    A.   crucial or acute
    B.   chronic
    C.   pre-alcoholic
    D.   warning

13. The difference between the effective dose level of a drug and the lowest toxic dose is   13.____
    expressed as the

    A.   Orange Book value
    B.   margin of safety
    C.   therapeutic index
    D.   therapeutic equivalence

14. Generally, "moderate" drinking is defined as no more than _____ drink(s) a day for   14.____
    women and _____ drink(s) a day for men.

    A.   1/2; 1   B.   1; 2
    C.   2; 3   D.   2; 4

15. Studies have demonstrated a cross-tolerance between LSD and   15.____

    A.   mescaline   B.   MDMA (ecstasy)
    C.   scopolamine   D.   harmaline

16. Which of the following opiates is the most potent?   16.____

    A.   Heroin   B.   Morphine
    C.   Fentanyl   D.   Codeine

17. Naltrexone, a drug used in the treatment of alcoholism, acts by   17.____

    A.   breaking alcohol down into separate molecules before it enters the bloodstream
    B.   decreasing the pleasure associated with alcohol use
    C.   mimicking the effects of alcohol in the brain, but with a lower intensity and duration
    D.   causing the user to become ill if alcohol is ingested

18. Drug use is proportionately more common among

    A. ethnic minorities
    B. the upper class
    C. the lower classes
    D. middle-class males

18.____

19. Which of the following is an appropriate "exit result" for an abuse prevention program?

    A. A short-term effect
    B. A long-term effect
    C. A strategy for insuring and measuring success
    D. Evidence that the program is working

19.____

20. The determination of whether a person's use of a substance become "abuse" is most clearly linked to

    A. the number of times a person uses drugs in any given time period
    B. a pattern in which repeated use becomes connected to undesirable consequences
    C. the amount of the substance the user takes at any given time
    D. whether the person moves on to use illicit drugs

20.____

21. Kaposi's sarcoma is a form of cancer that has been linked to the habitual inhalation of

    A. ether
    C. petroleum distillates
    B. nitrites
    D. toluene

21.____

22. A child with one alcoholic parent has about a _____ percent chance of becoming an alcoholic him/herself.

    A. 33
    C. 65
    B. 50
    D. 80

22.____

23. The likelihood of alcohol use _____ is most likely to be determined by cultural factors.

    A. resulting in aggressive behavior
    B. reducing stress
    C. affecting the liver
    D. acting on the "pleasure pathway" of the brain

23.____

24. The substances known as endorphins, which are produced naturally in the brain and pituitary gland, are most like _____ their composition and effect.

    A. opiates
    C. barbiturates
    B. stimulants
    D. benzodiazepines

24.____

25. Schedule III drugs include
    I. anabolic steroids
    II. benzodiazepines
    III. Vicodin
    IV. morphine

    A. I only
    C. II only
    B. I and III
    D. II and IV

25.____

KEY (CORRECT ANSWERS)

1.	C		11.	C
2.	A		12.	B
3.	B		13.	B
4.	C		14.	B
5.	C		15.	A
6.	A		16.	C
7.	B		17.	B
8.	C		18.	C
9.	A		19.	A
10.	D		20.	B

21.	B
22.	B
23.	A
24.	A
25.	B

TEST 3

DIRECTIONS: Each question or incomplete statement is followed by several suggested answers or completions. Select the one that BEST answers the question or completes the statement. *PRINT THE LETTER OF THE CORRECT ANSWER IN THE SPACE AT THE RIGHT.*

1. Alcohol breaks down in the body at a fairly constant rate of _____ ounce(s) per hour.　1.____

 A. 0.5 to 1.0　　　　　　　　B. 1.0 to 1.5
 C. 2 to 3　　　　　　　　　　D. 3 to 5

2. When the repeated intake of a substance leads to more enhanced effects, the phenomenon of sensitization, or _____, has occurred.　2.____

 A. reverse tolerance
 B. distributive effect
 C. cascading effect
 D. tolerance

3. A beverage that is "100 proof" contains _____ % alcohol　3.____

 A. 10　　　　　　　　　　　　B. 30
 C. 50　　　　　　　　　　　　D. 100

4. Marijuana is sometimes used medicinally to　4.____

 A. suppress appetite
 B. relieve intraocular (eye) pressure
 C. decrease heart rate
 D. dilate blood vessels

5. Of the following routes of administration, _____ results in the fastest delivery of a drug to the brain.　5.____

 A. ingestion　　　　　　　　　B. inhalation
 C. topically, on the skin　　　　D. topically, in the eye

6. Of the following drugs, the use of _____ most commonly results in addiction.　6.____

 A. heroin　　　　　　　　　　B. methamphetamine
 C. cocaine　　　　　　　　　　D. LSD

7. The most likely reaction to the ingestion of amphetamine is　7.____

 A. loss of appetite
 B. hallucination
 C. sedation
 D. increased alertness

8. The most notorious of the "designer drugs," originally created to get around existing drug laws by modifying their molecular structures, is　8.____

 A. rohypnol　　　　　　　　　B. ketamine
 C. psilocybin　　　　　　　　　D. ecstasy (MDMA)

9. Naltrexone is sometimes used to treat alcoholism by   9.____

    A. reducing the craving for alcohol
    B. blocking the reception of alcohol by brain receptors
    C. reversing the effects of alcohol intoxication
    D. producing an immediate and severe negative reaction to alcohol intake

10. Of the following, which is a hallucinogen that is extremely dangerous in high doses?   10.____

    A. Phencyclidine (PCP)
    B. Mescaline
    C. Psilocybin
    D. LSD

11. "Crack" is a purified form of _____ that produces a rapid and intense reaction in the user.   11.____

    A. methamphetamine   B. cocaine
    C. marijuana   D. heroin

12. Which of the following hallucinogens is taken by ingesting mushrooms in which it naturally occurs?   12.____

    A. Psilocybin   B. Mescaline
    C. LAA (lysergic acid amide)   D. Datura

13. Which of the following approaches to drug dependence treatment is based on the idea that dependence is best treated by intensive individual and group counseling, in either a residential or non-residential setting?   13.____

    A. Therapeutic community
    B. Structural/functional
    C. Aversion therapy
    D. Medical treatment

14. Which of the following is a danger that is specific to the abuse of ether?   14.____

    A. Long-term tissue retention
    B. Powerful hallucinations
    C. Ocular damage
    D. High flammability

15. "Black tar" is a street term for an inexpensive form of   15.____

    A. heroin   B. cocaine
    C. marijuana   D. MDMA (ecstasy)

16. Which of the following is most often classified by itself because it is technically more than one drug, with a wide range of effects?   16.____

    A. MDMA (ecstasy)   B. Marijuana
    C. GHB   D. LSD

17. Drugs that are classified as Schedule II by the DEA are said to have an accepted medical use in the United States, and a high liability for abuse. Examples include each of the following, EXCEPT

    A. methadone   B. ketamine
    C. pentobarbital   D. diazepam

17.____

18. The Pure Food and Drug Act, which required that all drugs be accurately labeled, was passed in

    A. 1888   B. 1906
    C. 1934   D. 1970

18.____

19. Company-sponsored drug abuse prevention programs generally have the greatest impact on businesses in the _____ sector.

    A. transportation
    B. health care
    C. telecommunications
    D. textile

19.____

20. Which of the following is most clearly classified as a stimulant?

    A. Morphine   B. Cocaine
    C. Alcohol   D. Marijuana

20.____

21. The Fourth Edition of the Diagnostic and Statistical Manual of Mental Disorders-commonly known as the DSM-IV and published by the American Psychiatric Association-lists each of the following as a possible psychiatric diagnosis, EXCEPT

    A. substance dependence   B. substance abuse
    C. alcoholism   D. cannabis delirium

21.____

22. The primary risk associated with the medical model for managing alcohol withdrawal is

    A. the development of a dependence on a new substance
    B. seizure
    C. abnormal heart rhythm
    D. a de-emphasis on the psychological factors that led to abuse

22.____

23. _____ prevention programs are aimed at people who have tried a certain drug or other drugs, but have not been treated for dependence

    A. Primary   B. Secondary
    C. Tertiary   D. Quaternary

23.____

24. Most of the money-from all sources-used in the United States to fight the problem of substance abuse is allocated to

    A. reducing the supply
    B. treatment programs
    C. law enforcement
    D. prevention programs

24.____

25. Alcohol contains
  - I. vitamins
  - II. calories
  - III. minerals
  - IV. proteins

A. I and II   B. II only
C. I and III   D. I, II, III and IV

25.____

———

KEY (CORRECT ANSWERS)

1.	A		11.	B
2.	A		12.	A
3.	C		13.	A
4.	B		14.	D
5.	B		15.	A
6.	A		16.	B
7.	D		17.	D
8.	D		18.	B
9.	A		19.	A
10.	A		20.	B

21.	C
22.	A
23.	B
24.	C
25.	B

———

TEST 4

DIRECTIONS: Each question or incomplete statement is followed by several suggested answers or completions. Select the one that BEST answers the question or completes the statement. *PRINT THE LETTER OF THE CORRECT ANSWER IN THE SPACE AT THE RIGHT.*

1. E.M. Jellinek's theory of alcoholism was that it was a(n)

    A. form of neurosis
    B. progressive disease that moved through several predictable stages
    C. form of deviance similar to other forms of insanity
    D. condition that arose directly as a result of one's home environment

1.____

2. The lifetime prevalence of alcohol dependence (the percentage of people who are alcoholics at any point in their lives) in the United States is about _____ percent.

    A. 6   B. 12
    C. 18   D. 25

2.____

3. Which of the following is NOT likely to be caused by chronic marijuana use?

    A. Impaired ability to learn
    B. Diminished motivation to work
    C. Aggressive behavior
    D. Decreased testosterone levels in men

3.____

4. "Hallucinogenic persisting perceptive disorder" is a clinical term for

    A. Formication   B. Eye twitches
    C. Flashback   D. Euphoria

4.____

5. Cocaine works by increasing the availability of _____ in the brain.

    A. acetylcholine   B. serotonin
    C. epinephrine   D. dopamine

5.____

6. Another term by which the opioid drugs are known is

    A. sedatives   B. barbiturates
    C. hypnotics   D. narcotics

6.____

7. Of the following substances, which is classified as both a hallucinogen and a stimulant?

    A. Cocaine   B. Ecstasy (MDMA)
    C. Heroin   D. Mescaline

7.____

8. In the year _____, the federal Food and Drug Administration began to require that new drugs had to be demonstrated to be effective before they could be marketed.

    A. 1906   B. 1912
    C. 1962   D. 1970

8.____

9. Accepted therapeutic uses of opiates include each of the following, EXCEPT

    A. cough suppression
    B. treatment of liver insufficiency
    C. treatment of severe diarrhea
    D. pain relief

9.____

10. Symptoms associated with heroin withdrawal include each of the following, EXCEPT   10._____

    A. muscle and bone pain
    B. vomiting
    C. cold sweats
    D. abdominal cramps

11. A drug introduced through IM injection will be absorbed most rapidly if injected into the   11._____

    A. deltoid   B. abdominals
    C. quadriceps   D. gluteals

12. When two drugs are present in the system at one time, but the effect of one reduces or   12._____
blocks the effect of the other, it is said to have a(n) _____ effect.

    A. potentiating   B. withdrawal
    C. inhibiting   D. synergistic

13. A(n) _____ prevention program is oriented to those who have already been treated for   13._____
substance abuse.

    A. primary   B. secondary
    C. tertiary   D. outpatient

14. Increased heart rate and blood pressure as the result of taking a drug are examples of   14._____
_____ activation.

    A. somatic   B. peripheral
    C. parasympathetic   D. sympathetic

15. Mescaline and psilocybin belong to the _____ class of drugs.   15._____

    A. hallucinogen   B. narcotic
    C. stimulant   D. depressant

16. The primary behavioral consequences of marijuana use are associated with   16._____

    A. problem-solving
    B. impulse control
    C. memory and attention
    D. sleep and dreams

17. The "flushing syndrome" associated with alcohol use typically involves each of the follow-   17._____
ing symptoms, EXCEPT

    A. memory problems
    B. hives
    C. headache
    D. rapid heart rate

18. Deliriant, or anticholinergic, drugs include   18._____

    A. ketamine   B. nitrous oxide
    C. datura   D. psilocybin

19. "Distilled spirits" or "hard liquor" generally has an alcohol content of about _____ per-   19._____
    cent

    A. 3.2 to 12.0   B. 15 to 30
    C. 40 to 50   D. 60 to 80

20. Which of the following is generally NOT an effect of chronic marijuana use?   20._____

    A. Lower infant birth weight
    B. Lower fertility for women
    C. Damage to the respiratory system
    D. Lowered sperm count in men

21. Currently, the preferred confirmatory test for the presence of alcohol and drugs is   21._____

    A. spectrophotometry
    B. radioimmunoassay
    C. gas chromatography/mass spectrometry (GC/MS)
    D. thin layer chromatography

22. Which of the following is a term for the state arising from alcohol abuse in which a person   22._____
    has difficulties in problem-solving, organizing facts about one's identity and environment,
    and remembering information?

    A. Alcoholic dementia
    B. Potentiation
    C. Alcoholic cirrhosis
    D. Alcoholic aphasia

23. Feelings of euphoria associated with the use of most inhalants tend to last about   23._____

    A. 40 seconds   B. 10 minutes
    C. one hour   D. 4 hours

24. A habitual marijuana user has discovered that he needs to smoke three times as much to   24._____
    achieve the level of intoxication he achieved a year ago.
    This phenomenon is known as

    A. withdrawal   B. potentiation
    C. reversion   D. tolerance

25. Drugs that are classified as Schedule I by the DEA are said to have no accepted medical   25._____
    use in the United States, and have a high liability for abuse. Examples of Schedule I
    drugs include each of the following, EXCEPT

    A. marijuana   B. mescaline
    C. morphine   D. heroin

KEY (CORRECT ANSWERS)

1.	B	11.	A
2.	B	12.	C
3.	C	13.	C
4.	C	14.	D
5.	D	15.	A
6.	D	16.	C
7.	B	17.	A
8.	C	18.	C
9.	B	19.	C
10.	D	20.	B

21.	C
22.	A
23.	C
24.	D
25.	C

EXAMINATION SECTION
TEST 1

DIRECTIONS: Each question or incomplete statement is followed by several suggested answers or completions. Select the one that BEST answers the question or completes the statement. *PRINT THE LETTER OF THE CORRECT ANSWER IN THE SPACE AT THE RIGHT.*

1. Which of the following benzodiazepines is treated most strictly by the federal government?

   A. Flunitrazepam (Rohypnol)
   B. Diazepam (Valium)
   C. Chlordiazepoxide (Librium)
   D. Alprazolam (Xanax)

   1._____

2. Which of the following neurotransmitters generally governs a person's wakefulness and arousal, and is involved in the "fight or flight" response?

   A. Acetylcholine
   B. Norepinephrine
   C. Dopamine
   D. Serotonin

   2._____

3. Another name for anticholinergic substances is

   A. dissociatives
   B. deliriants
   C. cannabinoids
   D. hormones

   3._____

4. Which of the following terms is used to denote efforts to halt the import, sale, and manufacture of illicit drugs?

   A. Narcoterrorism
   B. Diversion
   C. Customs
   D. Interdiction

   4._____

5. The psychoactive substance found in the peyote cactus is

   A. ketamine
   B. mescaline
   C. phencyclidine
   D. psilocybin

   5._____

6. Drugs that are used to treat the symptoms of alcoholic withdrawal include
   I. Librium
   II. phenobarbital
   III. methadone
   IV. disulfiram

   A. I and II   B. II only   C. II,III and IV   D. I, II, III and IV

   6._____

7. Which of the following drugs is used to stabilize the chemical balance of the brain, which would otherwise be disrupted by alcoholism?

    A. Acaraprosate (Campral)
    B. Naltrexone
    C. Baclofen
    D. Disulfiram (Antabuse)

7.___

8. Marijuana is known to affect the _____ , or the part of the brain that controls memory.

    A. cerebellum
    B. hippocampus
    C. pons
    D. hypothalamus

8.___

9. The most common cause of impotence among middle-aged men is

    A. overuse of stimulants
    B. nicotine addiction
    C. high blood pressure
    D. alcohol overuse

9.___

10. In medicine, narcotic analgesics are favored over other types of painkillers because they involve fewer adverse affects on

    A. the synaptic response
    B. the gastrointestinal system
    C. memory
    D. intellectual and motor function

10.___

11. A person's perception and judgement can be affected by moderate amounts of alcohol in each of the following ways, EXCEPT

    A. impaired sexual performance
    B. enhanced olfactory perception
    C. a diminished sensation of cold
    D. motor skill impairment

11.___

12. Which of the following effects is MOST likely to be associated with anabolic steroid abuse?

    A. loss of appetite
    B. elevated sperm count
    C. decreased blood pressure
    D. increased levels of low-density lipoproteins (LDL) in the blood

12.___

13. "Poppers" is a slang term used to denote the inhalant

    A. amyl nitrite
    B. butane
    C. diethyl ether
    D. nitrous oxide

13.___

14. A person finds that she needs larger and larger doses of a drug to achieve intoxication or other desired effects. This person has developed 14._____

   A. psychological dependence
   B. a potentiating response
   C. a physical dependence
   D. hypersensitivity to the drug

15. Which of the following is NOT a common side effect of antipsychotics? 15._____

   A. Dystonia
   B. Parkinsonism
   C. Impotence
   D. Cardiac arrhythmia

16. Which of the following terms is used to denote an enhanced, unpredictable effect caused by ingesting two or more substances? 16._____

   A. Covariance
   B. Synergism
   C. Stacking
   D. Tolerance

17. Insufflation is a technical term for the introduction of a drug by 17._____

   A. smoking
   B. suppository
   C. snorting
   D. using a skin patch

18. One criticism of the disease model for diagnosing and treating alcoholism is that 18._____

   A. it tends to stigmatize the individual who suffers from it
   B. it is too limited and should apply to other forms of behavioral intervention
   C. it calls upon the use of public resources to treat what is essentially an individual disorder
   D. the terminology seems to discount the individual's role in the process of addiction and treatment

19. Which of the following substances are naturally released by the brain when a person feels stress or pain? 19._____

   A. Endorphins
   B. GABA
   C. Carbon monoxide
   D. Morphine

20. Which of the following has been identified as a factor that may significantly reduce the likelihood of drug abuse? 20._____

   A. Strong family ties
   B. High socioeconomic status
   C. Race
   D. Higher level of education completed

21. When marijuana is smoked, it generally takes _____ for its psychoactive substance to reach the brain.

    A. a few seconds
    B. 30-45 seconds
    C. 2-3 minutes
    D. 5-8 minutes

21.___

22. Of the following processes, which produces the highest alcohol content?

    A. cold-filtering
    B. fermentation
    C. distillation
    D. brewing

22.___

23. Which of the following is a sympathomimetic effect?

    A. Constricted bronchial passages
    B. Constricted blood vessels
    C. Nausea
    D. Reduced cardiac output

23.___

24. Which of the following is an irreversible consequence of chronic alcohol abuse?

    A. Hepatitis
    B. Cirrhosis
    C. Pancreatitis
    D. Fatty liver

24.___

25. Historically, about _____ percent of heroin addicts have been able to break their addiction.

    A. 10
    B. 25
    C. 40
    D. 55

25.___

KEY (CORRECT ANSWERS)

1.	A		11.	B
2.	B		12.	D
3.	B		13.	A
4.	D		14.	C
5.	B		15.	D
6.	A		16.	B
7.	A		17.	C
8.	B		18.	D
9.	D		19.	A
10.	D		20.	A

21.	A
22.	C
23.	B
24.	B
25.	A

TEST 2

DIRECTIONS: Each question or incomplete statement is followed by several suggested answers or completions. Select the one that BEST answers the question or completes the statement. *PRINT THE LETTER OF THE CORRECT ANSWER IN THE SPACE AT THE RIGHT.*

1. Typically, alcohol first produces noticeable cognitive changes at a blood alcohol concentration (BAC) of

    A. .02% to .03%
    B. .05% to .08%
    C. .10% to. 15%
    D. .16% to .20%

1.___

2. The most common class of drugs used to treat the symptoms of those undergoing alcohol detoxification are the

    A. analgesics
    B. benzodiazepines
    C. amphetamines
    D. opiates

2.___

3. The most common reason for young people to try illegal drugs is

    A. emotional turmoil
    B. negative reinforcement
    C. curiosity
    D. peer pressure

3.___

4. About _____ percent of those who are classified as "heavy" marijuana users go on to use cocaine.

    A. 10
    B. 35
    C. 50
    D. 75

4.___

5. The slang term "chronic" is used to denote a potent form of marijuana, or marijuana laced with

    A. heroin
    B. ecstasy (MDMA)
    C. cocaine
    D. LSD

5.___

6. The ingestion of alcohol is followed by the release of _____ in the brain.
    I. dopamme
    II. serotonin
    III. norephinephrine
    IV. endorphins

    A. I and II
    B. I, II and III
    C. III and IV
    D. I, II, III and IV

6.___

7. _____ drinking is classified as drinking up to three or four standard alcoholic drinks in a day, no more than three days a week.

    A. Social
    B. Moderate
    C. Problem
    D. Binge

7.____

8. Widespread methamphetamine abuse in the United States is generally thought to have begun in

    A. the Midwest
    B. the South
    C. the West
    D. New England

8.____

9. The term _____ is used to describe people who have both a drug problem and a psychiatric disorder.

    A. dual diagnosis
    B. compound disorder
    C. bipolar
    D. differential diagnosis

9.____

10. Which of the following common household substances can—in massive doses—cause visual and auditory hallucinations?

    A. Banana peels
    B. Nutmeg
    C. Tomatoes
    D. Ginger

10.____

11. The use of cocaine in the United States peaked between the years

    A. 1920 and 1925
    B. 1940 and 1945
    C. 1960 and 1970
    D. 1980 and 1990

11.____

12. By definition, an analgesic is a drug that is designed to

    A. relieve pain by inducing unconsciousness
    B. stimulate the central nervous system
    C. relieve pain by stimulating a natural release of endorphins
    D. relieve pain without causing a loss of consciousness

12.____

13. Creatine is most accurately classified as a(n)

    A. vitamin
    B. drug
    C. nutritional supplement
    D. steroid

13.____

14. Substances commonly considered to be "gateway" drugs include each of the following, EXCEPT

    A. nicotine
    B. caffeine
    C. marijuana
    D. alcohol

14.___

15. Which of the following inhalants are typically inhaled out of paper or plastic bags?

    A. Oxides
    B. Solvents
    C. Nitrites
    D. Ether

15.___

16. Research based on the lives of twins has suggested that the heritability of alcohol abuse is about _____ percent,

    A. 10-25
    B. 30-40
    C. 50-60
    D. 70-85

16.___

17. Each of the following drugs causes withdrawal symptoms, EXCEPT

    A. marijuana
    B. alcohol
    C. caffeine
    D. ibuprofen

17.___

18. For nearly all of the drags of abuse, the "site of action" is the

    A. central nervous system
    B. physical location where the drug enters the body
    C. particular receptor where the substance prevents or accelerates the uptake of a certain neurotransmitter
    D. peripheral nervous system

18.___

19. Which of the following neurotransmitters plays an important role in emotional, mental, and motor functions?

    A. Endorphin
    B. Glutamate
    C. Serotonin
    D. Dopamine

19.___

20. Most hallucinogenic drugs are

    A. found in the natural environment
    B. Schedule III drugs
    C. synthetics
    D. legal

20.___

21. A teenager takes some of her mother's anti-anxiety medication to contend with the stress of final examinations. This is an example of _____ use.

    A. socio-recreational
    B. experimental
    C. circumstantial-situational
    D. intensified

21._____

22. When methadone is administered to avoid the withdrawal symptoms associated with heroin, it is administered

    A. hourly
    B. twice a day
    C. daily
    D. three times a week

22._____

23. The route of administration that introduces drugs into the bloodstream the fastest is

    A. intramuscular injection
    B. snorting
    C. smoking or inhaling into lungs
    D. intravenous injection

23._____

24. A common feature of fetal alcohol syndrome is _____ deformities.

    A. digital
    B. intestinal
    C. facial
    D. cardiac

24._____

25. The part of the brain that controls the emotional response is the

    A. pons
    B. limbic system
    C. hypothalamus
    D. reticular activating system

25._____

KEY (CORRECT ANSWERS)

1.	A		11.	B
2.	B		12.	D
3.	D		13.	C
4.	D		14.	B
5.	C		15.	B
6.	B		16.	C
7.	B		17.	D
8.	C		18.	A
9.	A		19.	D
10.	B		20.	A

21.	C
22.	C
23.	D
24.	C
25.	B

———

TEST 3

DIRECTIONS: Each question or incomplete statement is followed by several suggested answers or completions. Select the one that BEST answers the question or completes the statement. *PRINT THE LETTER OF THE CORRECT ANSWER IN THE SPACE AT THE RIGHT.*

1. Treatment for substance abuse is often considered to be a form of _____ prevention.   1._____

    A. primary
    B. secondary
    C. tertiary
    D. compound

2. Which of the following substances generally involves the LOWEST degree of physical dependence?   2._____

    A. LSD
    B. Valium
    C. Alcohol
    D. Methadone

3. Each of the following is a Schedule I drug, EXCEPT   3._____

    A. MDMA (ecstasy)
    B. GHB
    C. Cocaine
    D. LSD

4. Which of the following substances is known by the slang term "knockout drops"?   4._____

    A. Ketamine
    B. Ether
    C. Flunitrazepam (Rohypnol)
    D. Chloral hydrate

5. The most frequently committed crime in the United States is   5._____

    A. drinking underage
    B. underage purchase of alcohol
    C. driving while intoxicated
    D. illegal drug use

6. The word "psychotropic" is most accurately defined as   6._____

    A. addictive
    B. mind-altering
    C. hallucinatory
    D. mind-affecting

7. Which of the following causes of death is LEAST likely to be associated with the use of inhalants?   7._____

    A. respiratory depression   B. hypoxia
    C. cardiac arrest   D. aspiration of vomit

8. Physical dependence on a substance is indicated by the presence of   8.___

    A. denial
    B. withdrawal symptoms
    C. agonists
    D. psychological symptoms

9. Which of the following terms is used to denote the condition of a loss of contact with reality?   9.___

    A. Sociopathy
    B. Psychosis
    C. Personality disorder
    D. Neurosis

10. Which of the following is LEAST likely to be a condition that accompanies cocaine dependence?   10.___

    A. Heart failure
    B. Stroke
    C. Paranoia
    D. Irrepressible sex drive

11. More than any other drug, _____ is known for being taken in common with other recreational drugs.   11.___

    A. marijuana
    B. amphetamine
    C. ecstasy (MDMA)
    D. cocaine

12. Stage II of alcoholic withdrawal is characterized by   12.___

    A. convulsions
    B. rapid heartbeat
    C. hallucinations
    D. delirium

13. One of the earliest proponents of the therapeutic properties of cocainewas   13.___

    A. Sigmund Freud
    B. Everett Koop
    C. Timothy Leary
    D. King James I of England

14. Phencyclidine (PCP) tends to accumulate in   14.___

    A. the pancreas
    B. the liver
    C. extracellular fluid
    D. body fat

15. Which of the following neurotransmitters plays a significant role in regulating pain, eating, perception, and sleep?

    15.____

    A. Dopamine
    B. Epinephrine
    C. Serotonin
    D. GABA

16. Common symptoms of marijuana use include each of the following, EXCEPT

    16.____

    A. bloodshot eyes
    B. dry mouth
    C. increased intracranial pressure
    D. increased heart rate

17. Which of the following is NOT a sub-category of the class of drugs known as hallucinogens?

    17.____

    A. Deliriants
    B. Psychedelics
    C. Hypnotics
    D. Dissociatives

18. Research has indicated that women who are problem drinkers

    18.____

    A. have less risk for liver damage than men who are problem drinkers
    B. are at a much higher risk for osteoporosis than women who are not heavy drinkers
    C. are less likely to have an alcoholic parent than male problem drinkers
    D. are usually smokers as well

19. Of all the cases of pancreatitis that develop in the United States in a given year, about _____ % are thought to be caused by the use of alcohol.

    19.____

    A. 16-25
    B. 26-35
    C. 46-55
    D. 66-75

20. Today, the most acceptable and available treatment for heroin addicts is

    20.____

    A. the methadone maintenance program
    B. electroshock therapy
    C. group therapy
    D. a 12-step program similar to Alcoholics Anonymous

21. A person who is described as a compulsive drug user is likely to use drugs in order to

    21.____

    A. achieve pleasure
    B. avoid discomfort
    C. satisfy curiosity
    D. fit in with peers

22. The primary ingredient in most over-the-counter stimulants is   22.___

    A. nicotine
    B. caffeine
    C. diphenhydramine
    D. amphetamine

23. The peripheral nervous system is composed of the _____ and the _____ nervous sys-   23.___
tems.

    A. somatic; autonomic
    B. limbic; spinal
    C. sympathetic; parasympathetic
    D. central; enteric

24. When snorted, cocaine takes about _____ to reach the brain.   24.___

    A. 10-15 seconds
    B. 1-5 minutes
    C. 10-15 minutes
    D. 30-45 minutes

25. Of the following, the best predictor of alcoholism is   25.___

    A. genetic predisposition
    B. level of education achieved
    C. peer pressure
    D. socioeconomic status

KEY (CORRECT ANSWERS)

1.	C		11.	C
2.	A		12.	C
3.	C		13.	A
4.	D		14.	D
5.	C		15.	C
6.	D		16.	C
7.	C		17.	C
8.	B		18.	B
9.	B		19.	D
10.	D		20.	A

21.	B
22.	B
23.	A
24.	C
25.	A

TEST 4

DIRECTIONS: Each question or incomplete statement is followed by several suggested answers or completions. Select the one that BEST answers the question or completes the statement. *PRINT THE LETTER OF THE CORRECT ANSWER IN THE SPACE AT THE RIGHT.*

1. Each of the following is a risk factor that makes drug use more likely, EXCEPT

    A. a caregiver who abuses drugs
    B. poor family relations
    C. poor classroom behavior
    D. low socioeconomic status

1.____

2. The key characteristic that distinguishes hypnotic drugs from sedatives is that hypnotics are

    A. sometimes prescribed to relieve anxiety
    B. used to induce sleep
    C. prescribed to relieve pain
    D. controlled substances

2.____

3. Which of the following is NOT one of the four characteristic symptoms of addiction?

    A. Loss of control
    B. Negative consequences
    C. Compulsion to use the substance
    D. Recognition of the problem

3.____

4. The second dose or drink often does not have as great an effect as the first—an illustration of _____ tolerance.

    A. psychological   B. acute   C. behavior   D. reverse

4.____

5. One of the risks of amyl nitrite abuse is

    A. memory problems   B. flashbacks
    C. stroke   D. angina pectoris

5.____

6. The first barbiturate to be synthesized and commercially marketed was

    A. barbital   B. pento barbital
    C. secobarbital   D. methohexital

6.____

7. Which of the following drugs, first synthesized in 1874, was considered a wonder drug for the relief of pain?

    A. Aspirin   B. Laudanum   C. Cocaine   D. Heroin

7.____

8. Of the following, the class of drugs most often associated with anxiolytic (anxiety-reducing) properties is

    A. narcotics
    B. benzodiazepines
    C. hallucinogens
    D. barbiturates

8.____

9. In the United States, illicit drug use has a high correlation with   9.__

   A. depression
   B. race
   C. antisocial behavior
   D. socioeconomic status

10. A person's vital functions are regulated by the   10.__

    A. thalamus
    B. pituitary gland
    C. brain stem
    D. hippocampus

11. What is the term for a drug that is used to block the effects of narcotics?   11.__

    A. Agonist   B. Inhibitor   C. Antagonist   D. Methadone

12. A substance that reduces the effects mediated by acetylcholine in the central nervous   12.__
    system and the peripheral nervous system is a(n)

    A. hallucinogen
    B. benzodi azepi ne
    C. agonist
    D. anticholinergic

13. The first state to eliminate penalties for the medical use of marijuana was   13.__

    A. Alaska   B. California   C. Massachusetts   D. Oregon

14. In its effect on the central nervous system, amphetamine is very similar to   14.__

    A. marijuana   B. nicotine   C. cocaine   D. heroin

15. The psychoactive agent in glue that is sniffed or inhaled is   15.__

    A. toluene
    B. alkyl nitrite
    C. acetone
    D. xylene

16. Which of the following is a Schedule II drag?   16.__

    A. Heroin
    B. Benzodiazepines
    C. Phenobarbital
    D. Ritalin

17. At the beginning of the 21st century, alcohol was a factor in about _____ percent of traf-   17.__
    fic deaths in the United States.

    A. 20
    B. 40
    C. 60
    D. 80

18. Of the following, the stimulant most likely to be used illegally by college students in the early 21st century was

    18.____

    A. cocaine
    B. methamphetamine
    C. ecstasy (MDMA)
    D. Ritalin

19. The type of drinking most often practiced by college students is _____ drinking.

    19.____

    A. social
    B. binge
    C. moderate
    D. light

20. For many alcoholics, the first sign of alcohol-induced liver problems is

    20.____

    A. hypertension
    B. fatty liver
    C. cirrhosis
    D. cellular edema

21. Drug addiction is typically distinguished from misuse or abuse by _____ factors.

    21.____

    A. psychological
    B. criminal
    C. spiritual
    D. physical

22. Which of the following substances generally involves the HIGHEST degree of psychological dependence?

    22.____

    A. Seconal
    B. Methadone
    C. LSD
    D. Methamphetamine

23. The highest rate of alcohol consumption in the United States is among

    23.____

    A. adolescents
    B. young and middle-aged adults
    C. women
    D. the elderly

24. Which of the following has both hallucinogenic and anesthetic properties?

    24.____

    A. Phencyclidine (PCP)
    B. Mescaline
    C. LSD
    D. Marijuana

25. At the beginning of the 21st century, the largest cocaine-producing country in the world was

    25.____

    A. Colombia
    C. Mexico
    B. Bolivia
    D. Afghanistan

KEY (CORRECT ANSWERS)

1. D	11. C
2. B	12. D
3. D	13. B
4. B	14. C
5. C	15. A
6. A	16. D
7. D	17. B
8. B	18. D
9. C	19. B
10. C	20. B

21. D
22. D
23. B
24. A
25. A

———

EXAMINATION SECTION
TEST 1

DIRECTIONS: Each question or incomplete statement is followed by several suggested answers or completions. Select the one that BEST answers the question or completes the statement. *PRINT THE LETTER OF THE CORRECT ANSWER IN THE SPACE AT THE RIGHT*

1. According to the federal government, the estimated annual economic cost of drug abuse in the United States is closest to

    A. $500 million
    B. $4 billion
    C. $180 billion
    D. $1.2 trillion

1._____

2. Which of the following is an anesthetic inhalant?

    A. Xylene
    B. Nitrous oxide
    C. Amyl nitrite
    D. Toluene

2._____

3. Short-term effects of marijuana use include

    A. reduced heart rate
    B. increased blood pressure
    C. bronchitis
    D. increased appetite

3._____

4. The first alkaloid ever isolated from the opium poppy was

    A. morphine
    B. codeine
    C. heroin
    D. methadone

4._____

5. In the United States, the most effective drug abuse prevention efforts have typically focused on

    A. peer and social influences
    B. real-life case studies
    C. worst-case scenarios
    D. legal rationales

5._____

6. Fatal consequences, although rare, are possible for those who suddenly stop their chronic use of_____ without medical supervision.
    I. barbiturates
    II. alcohol
    III. cocaine
    IV. heroin

6._____

A. I or II
B. II only
C. I, II or IV
D. I, II, III or IV

7. The use of drugs or alcohol to avoid withdrawal symptoms is an example of   7.____

    A. potentiation
    B. positive reinforcement
    C. negative tolerance
    D. negative reinforcement

8. The barbiturates are typically classified according to their   8.____

    A. duration of action
    B. potential for interaction with alcohol
    C. method of metabolism
    D. chemical structure

9. Which of the following is a club drag that stimulates the release of human growth hormone, and whose main ingredient is an industrial solvent?   9.____

    A. GHB (gamma hydroxybutyrate)
    B. GABA (ganima-aminobutyric acid)
    C. MDMA (ecstasy)
    D. Ketamine

10. Typically, heroin is about_____times stronger than morphine.   10.____

    A. 1-2
    B. 3-10
    C. 5-20
    D. 40

11. Among the following groups, the highest rates of illicit drug use are reported among   11.____

    A. construction workers
    B. physicians and nurses
    C. law enforcement officers
    D. social sendee professionals

12. It is estimated that about   percent of patients who suffer from a form of mental illness also have a substance abuse disorder.   12.____

    A. 10-20
    B. 25-35
    C. 40-75
    D. 70-85

13. The indirect effects of alcohol consumption are illustrated by the   13.____

    A. decrease in thiamin absorption
    B. increased risk of fetal alcohol syndrome among pregnant women

C.   relationship between drinking and motor vehicle crashes
D.   relationship between drinking and liver cancer

14.   Which of the following is classified as a deliriant?   14._____

A.   Psilocybin
B.   Mescaline
C.   Datura
D.   LSD

15.   Most first-time drinkers would likely be passed out by the time their blood alcohol content   15._____
reaches _____ %.

A.   .05
B.   .08
C.   .15
D.   .20

16.   Each of the following neurotransmitters is thought to play a role in a person's biological   16._____
predisposition toward alcoholism, EXCEPT

A.   GABA
B.   norepinephrine
C.   serotonin
D.   dopamine

17.   Typically, the alcohol in a drink will reach the bloodstream in about _____ minutes.   17._____

A.   15
B.   30
C.   45
D.   60

18.   Which of the following drugs is used to treat manic symptoms?   18._____

A.   Lithium
B.   Methadone
C.   Paxil
D.   Librium

19.   _____ drugs typically act by blocking the brain's dopamine receptors.   19._____

A.   Antipsychotic
B.   Steroidal
C.   Analgesic
D.   Opioid

20.   For U.S. adolescents in a substance treatment program, the primary drug of abuse is   20._____
most likely to be

A.   marijuana
B.   an inhalant
C.   alcohol
D.   cocaine

21. In 1988 the Anti-Drug Abuse Act created the government agency known as the
    - A. White House Office of National Drug Control Policy (ONDCP)
    - B. Substance Abuse and Mental Health Services Administration (SAMH-SA)
    - C. Drug Enforcement Agency (DEA)
    - D. National Institute on Drag Abuse (NIDA)

21. ___

22. Babies whose mothers have used cocaine during pregnancy are likely to have a higher rate of
    - I. low birth weight
    - II. sudden infant death syndrome (SIDS)
    - III. genito-urinary malformations
    - IV. congenital heart delects

    - A. I and II
    - B. IIand III
    - C. II and IV
    - D. I, II, III and IV

22. ___

23 A "Type I" alcoholic generally has each of the following personality traits, EXCEPT
    - A. optimism
    - B. rigidity in behaviors and beliefs
    - C. shyness
    - D. sentimentality

23. ___

24. Each of the following is a commonly occurring effect of chronic opiate dosing, EXCEPT
    - A. weightless
    - B. increased urination
    - C. constricted pupils
    - D. elevated body temperature

24. ___

25. The late stages of alcoholism are often characterized by
    - A. reverse tolerance
    - B. synergism
    - C. pharmacological tolerance
    - D. cross-tolerance

25. ___

KEY (CORRECT ANSWERS)

1.	C		11.	A
2.	B		12.	C
3.	D		13.	C
4.	A		14.	C
5.	A		15.	C
6.	C		16.	B
7.	D		17.	A
8.	A		18.	A
9.	A		19.	A
10.	B		20.	A

21.	A
22.	D
23.	A
24.	C
25.	A

TEST 2

DIRECTIONS: Each question or incomplete statement is followed by several suggested answers or completions. Select the one that BEST answers the question or completes the statement. *PRINT THE LETTER OF THE CORRECT ANSWER IN THE SPACE AT THE RIGHT.*

1. Alcohol withdrawal differs significantly from withdrawal from other drugs in that it   1.____

    A. can result in hallucinations
    B. is purely psychological
    C. can be directly fatal
    D. is treatable with synthetic opioids

2. Although the terms "opioid" and "opiate" are often used interchangeably, "opiate" more   2.____
properly refers only to

    A. opioids that are produced naturally by an organism
    B. natural opium alkaloids and the semi-synthetics derived from them.
    C. an opioid that is used only as prescribed
    D. fully synthetic opioids

3. Ingesting/injecting several anabolic steroids at once is referred to as   3.____

    A. stacking
    B. cycling
    C. chipping
    D. raging

4. Over the years, research has suggested that women who drink heavily die an average of   4.____
_____ years earlier than women who do not drink at all.

    A. 5
    B. 10
    C. 15
    D. 25

5. The first stage of barbiturate withdrawal, the "delirium" stage, lasts for about   5.____

    A. 12 hours
    B. 48 hours
    C. 5 days
    D. 10 days

6. NMDA receptor antagonists include   6.____
    I. PCP
    II. ketamine
    III. psilocybin
    IV. LSD

    A. I only
    B. I and II
    C. II and III
    D. LSD

7. Rebound insomnia, in which a person has greater difficulty falling asleep, is often associated with the use of

    A. stimulants
    B. sedative hypnotics
    C. hallucinogens
    D. narcotics

7.____

8. A single marijuana cigarette is associated with about _____ the bronchial damage associated with a regular tobacco cigarette.

    A. half
    B. the same
    C. 4 times
    D. 20 times

8.____

9. A drug that is described as "diuretic"

    A. softens the stool and makes defecation easier
    B. is used to treat heart arrhythmias
    C. accelerates the elimination of fluid
    D. slows the elimination of fluid

9.____

10. As of 2007, Rohypnol is a Schedule _____ substance.

    A. I
    B. II
    C. III
    D. IV

10.____

11. If a drug is said to have a therapeutic index of 1:4, that means that

    A. the effective dose is 1/4 of the lethal dose.
    B. only 1 person in 4 can safely use the drug.
    C. the drug remains effective for 1-4 hours.
    D. only 1/4 of the effective dose is biotransformed every hour.

11.____

12. Between a third and two-thirds of all child-welfare cases in the United States involve

    A. child substance abuse
    B. parental substance abuse
    C. prenatal substance exposure
    D. parental tobacco use

12.____

13. Methamphetanine is sometimes prescribed today for the treatment of

    A. atrial fibrillation
    B. insomnia
    C. depression
    D. attention deficit/hyperactivity disorder (ADHD)

13.____

14. Which of the following drug abuse prevention methods teaches students to recognize, manage, and avoid situations that might involve drug abuse?

14.____

A. Resistance skills training
B. Values clarification
C. Negative reinforcement
D. Self-efficacy training

15. In the United States, about _____ percent of all primary care and hospitalized patients suffer from alcohol dependence.   15.____

   A. 5 to 7
   B. 15 to 20
   C. 25 to 40
   D. 35 to 50

16. Which of the following is NOT a common sign of barbiturate use?   16.____

   A. Constricted pupils
   B. Cyanosis
   C. Cold, clammy skin
   D. Muscle twitches

17. In a given day, about _____ Americans receive treatment for alcoholism.   17.____

   A. 700,000
   B. 1.2 million
   C. 3.4 million
   D. 6 million

18. Drugs that are known for their relatively narrow therapeutic window, or margin of safety, include   18.____

   I. digoxin
   II. lithium carbonate
   III. opioids
   IV. acetaminophen

   A. I and II
   B. I, II and IV
   C. III only
   D. I, II and III

19. The class of drugs with the fewest accepted medical uses are the   19.____

   A. hallucinogens
   B. stimulants
   C. anabolic steroids
   D. opioids

20. Which of the following is most commonly associated with stroke, lung and liver damage, and sudden death due to cardiac arrest?   20.____

   A. Ketamine
   B. Ecstasy
   C. Marijuana
   D. Cocaine

21. Quaalude, a barbiturate alternative, is a brand name for the drug

    A. mefloquine
    B. quinine
    C. methaqualone
    D. quazepam

21. _____

22. The median lethal dose for alcohol is a blood alcohol content (BAC) of about _____ percent.

    A. .20
    B. .40
    C. .60
    D. .80

22. _____

23. Which of the following is a powerful opiate known by the slang term "China White"?

    A. Morphine
    B. Darvon
    C. Percocet
    D. Fentanyl

23. _____

24. When a person's average number of drinks per day are plotted on the horizontal axis of a graph, beginning with "zero" in the lower left corner, and the risk of death is plotted upward on the vertical axis, the result is a(n)

    A. J-shaped curve
    B. straight diagonal line traveling to the upper right
    C. M-shaped curve
    D. bell curve , "

24. _____

25. An example of a "harm reduction" policy approach to drug abuse is

    A. mandatory diversions
    B. needle-exchange programs
    C. education programs
    D. decriminalization

25. _____

KEY (CORRECT ANSWERS)

1.	C		11.	A
2.	B		12.	B
3.	A		13.	D
4.	C		14.	A
5.	C		15.	B
6.	B		16.	A
7.	B		17.	A
8.	D		18.	B
9.	C		19.	A
10.	D		20.	D

21.	C
22.	B
23.	D
24.	A
25.	B

——————

TEST 3

DIRECTIONS: Each question or incomplete statement is followed by several suggested answers or completions. Select the one that BEST answers the question or completes the statement. *PRINT THE LETTER OF THE CORRECT ANSWER IN THE SPACE AT THE RIGHT.*

1. In the United States, illicit drag use is most prevalent in   1.____

    A. inner city areas
    B. the suburbs
    C. rural areas
    D. the Midwest

2. The goal of the intervention process is to   2.____

    A. convince the person that he or she needs treatment
    B. identify the person's primary defense mechanism
    C. isolate the client to make him or her feel the consequences of behavior
    D. establish a working relationship with the physician or substance abuse counselor

3. Typically, about _____ percent of alcohol-dependent people seek treatment for their dis-   3.____
order.

    A. 10
    B. 25
    C. 35
    D. 50

4. The word "flip," in varying forms, is often used to describe a combination of the drug   4.____
_____ with another recreational drug.

    A. ecstasy (MDMA)
    B. cocaine
    C. LSD
    D. marijuana

5. Which of the following does NOT bind with the brain's serotonin receptors?   5.____

    A. LSD
    B. Haloperidol
    C. Psilocybin
    D. DMT

6. The Fourth Edition of the Diagnostic and Statistical Manual of Mental Disorderscom-   6.____
monly known as the DSM-IV and published by the American Psychiatric Associationin-
cludes each of the following in its criteria for a diagnosis of drug or alcohol dependency,
EXCEPT

    A. developing a tolerance for the substance
    B. preoccupation with further use of the substance
    C. using the substance solely in moments of peak stress
    D. using the substance at inappropriate times

7. Neurotransmitters is involved in the voluntary movement of muscles include   7.____
   - I. epinephrine
   - II. dopamine
   - III. acetylcholine
   - IV. GABA

   A. I and II
   B. II and III
   C. II, III and IV
   D. I, II, III and IV

8. The psychoactive agent in permanent markers that are sniffed or inhaled is   8.____

   A. acetone
   B. xylene
   C. ether
   D. butane

9. Minor tranquilizers, nonbarbiturate sedatives, and barbiturates are classified as   9.____

   A. sedative hypnotics
   B. psychedelics
   C. benzodiazepines
   D. inhalants

10. Other than methadone, which of the following is a synthetic drug approved for treating   10.____
    narcotic withdrawal?

    A. GHB
    B. Fentanyl
    C. LAAM
    D. Thiamine

11. The psychological trait most often linked with drug use is   11.____

    A. antisocial personality disorder
    B. low self-esteem
    C. impulsiveness
    D. denial

12. The smallest amount of a drug required to produce an effect is called the _____ dose.   12.____

    A. therapeutic
    B. standard
    C. threshold
    D. marginal

13. As a group, the ethnicity that typically records the lowest alcohol consumption in the   13.____
    United States is

    A. Asian Americans
    B. Hispanic Americans
    C. Euro-Americans
    D. African Americans

14. Injecting cocaine provides the highest blood levels of the drug in the shortest amount of time, but is generally avoided by users because it 14.____

    A. tends to cause immediate unconsciousness
    B. is very dangerous
    C. results in a loss of motor control
    D. tends to cause uncontrollable vomiting

15. Physiological symptoms associated with heroin use include 15.____
    I. vomiting
    II. sleepiness
    III. constipation
    IV. reduced sex drive

    A. I and II
    B. II only
    C. II and III
    D. I, II, III and IV

16. Each of the following has been classified as a psychedelic drug, EXCEPT 16.____

    A. Ketamine
    B. LSD
    C. marijuana
    D. ecstasy (MDMA)

17. During the hour after cocaine is used, the risk of heart attack increases by a factor of about 17.____

    A. 5
    B. 10
    C. 25
    D. 50

18. Tricyclic drags, when combined with _____ , may produce a fatal reaction. 18.____

    A. LSD
    B. benzodiazepines
    C. alcohol
    D. narcotics

19. Which of the following is NOT a health risk associated with alcoholism? 19.____

    A. Bladder cancer
    B. Pancreatitis
    C. Hypertension
    D. Breast cancer

20. Statistics show that most people in drug or alcohol treatment programs throughout the United States 20.____

    A. use primarily one drug of choice
    B. are unlikely to use again after completing the program

C. use more than one substance
D. are between the ages of 35 and 44

21. The age group most likely to abuse inhalants is

    A. 12-17
    B. 18-25
    C. 25-44
    D. 45-60

21.____

22. Under the Controlled Substances Act, benzodiazepines are Schedule _____ .

    A. I
    B. II
    C. III
    D. IV

22.____

23. A single drink containing one ounce (28 grams) of alcohol will increase the average person's BAC by roughly _____ percent.

    A. .01
    B. .03
    C. .05
    D. .07

23.____

24. Withdrawal from THC is commonly associated with each of the following, EXCEPT

    A. nausea
    B. paranoia
    C. insomnia
    D. loss of appetite

24.____

25. When a pregnant woman drinks alcohol, the fetal blood alcohol will equal the mother's in about

    A. 15 minutes
    B. 1 hour
    C. 3 hours
    D. 6 hours

25.____

KEY (CORRECT ANSWERS)

1.	A		11.	D
2.	A		12.	C
3.	A		13.	A
4.	A		14.	D
5.	B		15.	D
6.	C		16.	A
7.	C		17.	C
8.	B		18.	C
9.	A		19.	A
10.	C		20.	C

21. A
22. D
23. B
24. B
25. A

———————

TEST 4

DIRECTIONS: Each question or incomplete statement is followed by several suggested answers or completions. Select the one that BEST answers the question or completes the statement. *PRINT THE LETTER OF THE CORRECT ANSWER IN THE SPACE AT THE RIGHT.*

1. In the United States, about_____percent of the convicts housed in federal prisons are there because of drug-related crimes.

    A. 10
    B. 30
    C. 50
    D. 70

    1.____

2. Which of the following is NOT an opioid?

    A. Codeine
    B. Oxycodone
    C. Heroin
    D. Cocaine

    2.____

3. Marijuana is most likely to be used medically as a(n)

    A. anti-emetic
    B. laxative
    C. anti-inflammatory
    D. diuretic

    3.____

4. The brain's center of arousal and motivation, and attention is known as the

    A. reticular activating system
    B. limbic system
    C. frontal cortex
    D. basal ganglia

    4.____

5. Which of the following is a brand name for a benzodiazepine most commonly used to induce sleep?

    A. Xanax
    B. Valium
    C. Librium
    D. Halcion

    5.____

6. The class of drugs known as hypnotics typically includes
    I. GHB
    II. benzodiazepines
    III. opiates
    IV. barbiturates

    A. I and II
    B. I, III and IV
    C. II and IV
    D. I, II, III and IV

    6.____

7. It usually takes about _____ for inhaled drugs to reachthe brain.   7.____

    A. less than a second
    B. 5-8 seconds
    C. 20-30 seconds
    D. 1-3 minutes

8. What is the term for a chemical substance that crosses a synapse to a receptor site?   8.____

    A. Hormone
    B. Dendrite
    C. Neurotransmitter
    D. Agonist

9. Which of the following is NOT classified as a dissociative anesthetic drug?   9.____

    A. Psilocybin
    B. Ketamine
    C. Phencyclidine (PCP)
    D. Dextromethorphan

10. For at-risk students in the United States, the most effective drug abuse prevention programs are usually _____ in their approach.   10.____

    A. confrontational
    B. alternative
    C. highly structured
    D. peer-led

11. Heavy consumption of alcohol reduces the production of the neuroinhibito   11.____

    A. GABA
    B. glutamate
    C. glycine
    D. NDMA

12. In the United States of the early 21st century, the drug of abuse most likely to be administered intravenously was   12.____

    A. cocaine
    B. Flunitrazepam (Rohypnol)
    C. methamphetamine
    D. heroin

13. Of the following physical effects of narcotics, the LEAST common is   13.____

    A. dry mouth
    B. nausea
    C. respiratory depression
    D. constipation

14. The "controlled drinking" approach to treating alcoholism is not recommended for people with   14.____

A. little or no social support
B. functional problems related to alcoholism
C. liver disease
D. cancer

15. The route of administration for anabolic steroids that showed the largest growth in popularity during the early 21st century was

15.____

A. intravenous injection
B. intramuscular injection
C. creams, gels, and transdermal patches
D. oral ingestion

16. Of the following routes of administration, which is LEAST likely to lead to overdose?

16.____

A. Injecting
B. Smoking
C. Swallowing
D. Snorting

17. In the United States, a blood alcohol concentration reported as .20% means specifically that

17.____

A. every 100 milliliters of a person's blood contains .02 grams of alcohol
B. every 1000 grams of a person's blood contains 2 grams of alcohol
C. every 200 grams of a person's blood contains a milliliter of alcohol
D. every 1000 milliliters of a person's blood contains .02 milliliters of blood

18. The increasing use of inhalants by American teenagers has been largely attributed to

18.____

A. the low cost and availability of inhalants
B. a lack of clear regulation regarding their use
C. a celebrity culture that glorifies the use of inhalants
D. the increasing refinement of inhalants that produce euphoria

19. When abused, methamphetamines are especially harmful to the _____ system.

19.____

A. gastrointestinal
B. dental
C. autonomic nervous
D. cardiovascular

20. At the beginning of the 21st century, the world's largest producer of illegal opium was

20.____

A. Myanmar
B. Colombia
C. Afghanistan
D. China

21. Another term for antipsychotic drugs is

21.____

A. minor tranqui lizers
B. benzodiazepines

C. major tranquilizers
D. hypnotics

22. Chronic alcohol use affects the body's immune system in each of the following ways, EXCEPT by

    22.____

  A. increasing the susceptibility to infection
  B. inhibiting white blood cells
  C. interfering with recovery from colds and flu
  D. increasing red blood cell counts

23. Each of the following has been linked to steroid use, EXCEPT

    23.____

  A. Liver and kidney cancer
  B. Pancreatitis
  C. Low sperm count
  D. Abrupt mood swings

24. In the last half-century, the medical community has been most significantly influenced by the _____ model as the explanation for why people abuse alcohol.

    24.____

  A. social learning
  B. disease
  C. stress-response-dampening
  D. tension reduction

25. The Drug Abuse Warning Network (DAWN) is a system that

    25.____

  A. seeks to discourage interest in illegal drugs, gangs, and violence through education
  B. improves the quality and availability of prevention, treatment, and rehabilitative services in order to reduce illness, death, disability, and cost to society resulting from substance abuse and mental illness
  C. monitors drug-related visits to hospital emergency departments and drug-related deaths investigated by medical examiners and coroners
  D. establishes policies, priorities, and objectives to eradicate illicit drug use, manufacturing, and trafficking, drug-related crime and violence, and drug-related health consequences in the United States

KEY (CORRECT ANSWERS)

1. C	11. A
2. D	12. C
3. A	13. C
4. A	14. C
5. D	15. C
6. C	16. C
7. B	17. A
8. C	18. A
9. A	19. D
10. B	20. C

21. C
22. D
23. B
24. B
25. C

———————

BASIC FUNDAMENTALS OF ALCOHOL AND ALCOHOLISM

TABLE OF CONTENTS

BASIC FUNDAMENTALS OF
ALCOHOL AND ALCOHOLISM

INTRODUCTION

"We deal with alcohol -- cunning, baffling, powerful," says the "Big Book" of Alcoholics Anonymous.

So be it. But the cunning, bafflement and power have often been embellished, by those who exploit it for their own ends. "Grab for all the gusto you can get!" urges the beer advertisement. "There's death in the cup -- so beware!" warns the tectotalist.

As a result, so many prejudices and old wives tales have been fostered by alcohol and alcoholism that John Doe has found himself groping in a fog of misunderstanding.

The alcoholism counselor, if he is to function effectively, must cut through the smoke screens and camouflage. Only in that way can he distinguish the true from the false and win the confidence of his patients, their families and their associates. And once he feels reasonably informed, there will be new facts and findings to assimilate and adapt to as research keeps marching on.

I. ALCOHOL, THE BEVERAGE

The history of man's use of alcohol may be boiled down to two sentences. Historically, there is every evidence that man learned how to brew beer before he learned how to bake bread. Go we have had alcohol, the beverage, with us through the ages and will probably continue to have it to the end of time -- legislation and condemnation notwithstanding.

The alcohol contained in the beverage alcohol is called ethyl alcohol (C_2H_5OH), also known as ethanol. There are many other types of alcohol -- such as methyl or wood alcohol, isopropyl or rubbing alcohol, both unfit for human consumption.

First, to examine some popular misconceptions:

Alcohol is not a stimulant. On the contrary, it is an anesthetic. As explained in the next section, it puts judgment and inhibitions to sleep so that emotions and desires are allowed to function unrestrained, giving a false sense of stimulation.

Alcohol is not an aphrodisiac, it does not stimulate one's appetite for sex. Although one or two drinks may lower the individual's inhibitions and facilitate the expression of repressed sexual desires, in larger amounts alcohol -- being an anesthetic -- tends to curb sexual desire and, in the male, may even impair his ability to perform.

Alcohol is an addictive drug. As with all other addictive drugs, the excessive use of alcohol leads to an increased tolerance for it. In the early stages of the disease, the alcoholic can consume much more than the non-alcoholic. Also, withdrawal symptoms often occur with abstinence. One of the more widely known examples is delirium tremens. However, it must be stressed that, as with all other addictive drugs, not all users become addicted. In the case of alcohol, only about 6 to 7 per cent of all drinkers become alcoholics.

Alcohol does <u>not</u> necessarily stimulate one's appetite for food. As a sedative, alcohol taken in small quantity before a meal may help one "unwind" and thus add to his enjoyment of the food by temporarily alleviating his emotional frustrations and worries. Some drinks (aperitifs) contain substances (strychnine, quinine, etc.) specifically for the appetite stimulating effects. In larger amounts, it suppresses the appetite, because one ounce of alcohol supplies 200 calorics to the body. As a result, a heavy drinker may forego meals and rely on alcohol for his needed energy. But alcohol is a very poor substitute for food since it does not supply the proteins, vitamins and minerals necessary to good health.

Drinking in moderation does <u>not</u> in itself cause disease. But prolonged, excessive use of alcohol may lead to illnesses in several ways. They can be the direct result of the toxic effects of the drug on living tissue -- e.g., fatty deposits in the liver, heart muscle, etc. They can be the result of poor nutrition -- the lack of proteins, vitamins and minerals mentioned above. Or they can be the result of lowered resistance to infectious diseases -- i.e., the inhibition of the anti-body building, defense mechanisms of the body.

By itself, alcohol is <u>not</u> a killer. It is virtually impossible for a man to deliberately "drink himself to death." When the concentration of alcohol in the blood reaches .50 per cent, it affects the portion of the brain that controls breathing and heartbeat, and death follows. But the drinker loses consciousness when the concentration reaches .40 per cent, at which point he can drink no more.

There is no alcoholic "drink of moderation." Beer, wine, and spirits all contain alcohol. It may take more beer (4%) than 100 proof whiskey (50%) to reach the same state of intoxication. But the effect of the alcohol is the same. The "moderation" rests in the drinker.

II. <u>PHYSIOLOGICAL EFFECTS</u>

When one takes a drink -- be it man or woman, alcoholic or non-alcoholic -- the brain and body respond in a systematic manner.

About 10 percent of the alcohol is eliminated through the lungs, kidneys and pores of the skin. The remaining 90 percent is directly absorbed into the blood stream through the walls of the stomach and small intestine. No other digestive processes are involved.

Once in the blood stream, it is distributed to the body tissues.

En route, the alcohol passes through the liver, where it is oxidized and transformed into energy. But even a healthy liver can only oxidize about three-quarters of an ounce per hour. So the excess accumulates in the blood and continues to circulate.

In the blood, alcohol reaches the brain. Here it has a sedative and an anesthetic effect.

The first part of the brain to be affected is the frontal lobe of the cerebrum. This is the seat of reasoning, conscious thinking, memory, self-control. As the frontal lobe is gradually anesthetized by the alcohol, inhibitions disappear. The man forgets his limitations and becomes Mr. Big. No transient ambition is beyond his capacities. The anxieties of day-to-day living evaporate and the world is his friend. This is the false "stimulation" referred to before.

As the concentration of alcohol in the blood increases, other areas of the brain arc affected. The motor area of the cerebrum and the cerebellum control motor activity, muscular coordination and equilibrium. The drinker becomes clumsy and he begins to have trouble walking and keeping his balance. The speech, hearing and vision centers of the brain become affected, which result in slurred speech, dulled hearing and blurred vision. When the sensory area is affected the drinker "feels no pain," thus being deprived of a frequently lifesaving alarm system.

Finally, the medulla -- the portion of the brain connected to the spinal cord -- is affected. This is responsible for the vital functions of the body, including heartbeat, blood flow and breathing. Depending upon the concentration of the alcohol, the drinker will lose consciousness, go into shock, or die.

Thus a drinker's behavior and capabilities are directly related to the alcoholic concentration in his bloodstream. Such being the case, the drinking "capacity" of one man can vary from that of the next. The body fluids inside a 250-pound mailroom clerk. Other things being equal, more alcohol is required to raise the football player's concentration to .40%, or to any other given degree. So the amount of liquor considered "excessive" for one man may not be "excessive" for the next.

But football player or mailroom clerk, a drinker's behavior pattern generally conforms to the following levels of concentration:

.06% Feeling of warmth, relaxation, less concern with minor irritations.

.15% Abnormality of gross bodily function and mental facilities

.08% Legal point of intoxication

.30% Stupor

.09% Buoyancy, exaggerated emotion and behavior, talkative or morose.

.40% Unconsciousness, possible state of shock

.12% Impairment of fine coordination, slight to moderate unsteadiness in standing or walking.

.50% Death

There are, of course, other physiological effects resulting from drinking, many of which are noted below, under "Progressive Symptoms."

Both alcoholics and non-alcoholics, however, are liable to suffer irritation of the throat, esophagus and stomach lining through excessive drinking of undiluted liquors. Painful alcoholic gastritis can result from the latter

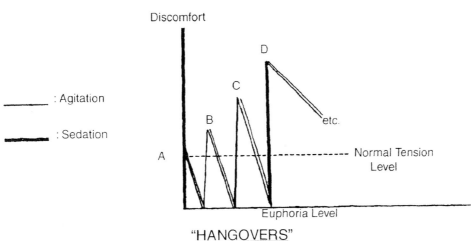

"HANGOVERS"

Then there is that transient hell through which any drinker can pass after he has imbibed too much "the hangover."

All sedatives, including alcohol, have a double-barreled effect. One is the tranquilizing effect which causes men and women to drink. The other is an irritating effect resulting in "psychomotor hyperactivity" which lasts many hours longer and which accounts for the "morning after" distress.

In the accompanying schematic diagram, assume that a man on his way to a party is somewhat nervous and normally anxious (point "A"). He takes a stiff drink to alleviate his anxiety and induce a sense of euphoria. At this stage the sedative effect of the alcohol is intense enough to mask the agitating effect. But within a relatively short period of time, the sedative effect of the alcohol is gone and he is left with only the psychomotor agitation, which gradually accelerates to point "B." He decides upon another drink to rectify matters. Now he needs even more sedation -- first, to get back to his normal state, and then more to become euphoric again. So the process of alternating sedation and agitation continues to points "C," "D" and so on -- until he either goes to bed himself or is carried there by his friends.

In actuality, the party-goer would surely refuel at the first suspicion that his euphoria was wearing off. But he would still awaken the following morning with an accumulation of the agitating effects of his drinks, which last about twelve hours from the time of imbibing. He has three choices: to sweat them out; to take a milder sedative to allay some of the pain; or to have some "hair bf the dog that bit him." The last is rather dangerous. He might find himself back on the same merry-go-round again.

III. ALCOHOLISM DEFINED

Thus far everything has applied to all the men and women who drink any alcoholic beverages at all.

What about the alcoholic? What about the 6 to 7 per cent of those drinkers -- the 1 out of 14 or 15 -- who have lost control of their drinking? What distinguishes them from the others?

There are hundreds of definitions of alcoholism. The technical one published by the World Health Organization reads as follows:

"Any form of drinking which in its extent goes beyond the traditional and customary 'dietary' use or the ordinary compliance with the social drinking customs of the whole community concerned, irrespective of the etiological factors leading to such behavior, and irrespective also of the extent to which such etiological factors are dependent upon heredity, constitution, or acquired physio-pathological and metabolic influences."

Shorter descriptions of the alcoholic include:

"One who repeatedly seeks to change reality through the use of alcohol."

Or

"One who suffers because of uncontrolled compulsive drinking."

For the alcoholism counselor, the following definition may serve as a useful yardstick in evaluating a client's status:

"An alcoholic is one whose drinking interferes with his health, his job, his relations with his family, or his community relationships and yet he continues to drink."

The interference need only be felt in one of the above areas of living for a person's classification as an alcoholic.

The fact that the alcoholic "continues to drink" implies loss of control, which is a characteristic of the illness.

The definition applies to men and women alike. Although it was once thought that male alcoholics outnumbered female alcoholics about five to one, it is now agreed that the number of women is much closer to that of men. Many private physicians who treat both men and women alcoholics say the ratio is about fifty-fifty.

And the definition applies to all social and economic "classes." Only 3 per cent of the alcoholics in the United States are found on Skid Row. The other 97 per cent stretch from waterfront saloons to Main Street and the Hall of Congress.

IV. ALCOHOLISM: TYPES

Since the alcoholic is usually the last to recognize his illness, he often challenges the doctor or counselor with:

"I only drink weekends (or paydays)!" or

"I can go months without touching a drop!" etc.

Such protests may be true. Nevertheless, he can still fall into one of the classifications of alcoholics that have been arrived at by many specialists in the field.

Probably the best known classification is that of the late Dr. E. M. Jellinek, former consultant to the World Health Organization. He identified various types of alcoholics with Greek letters:

Alpha: This man or woman relies upon the effect of alcohol to boost morale,
      bolster self-confidence or relieve emotional pain. He might be regarded as a "social drinker" except for the fact that he often drinks too much at the wrong times, among the wrong people, and is thereby apt to affront others.

The Alpha type does not lose control and can abstain when necessary. However, his drinking can give rise to family squabbles, occasional absenteeism from work, and be a drain on the family budget.

Alpha drinkers may develop into full-fledged Gamma alcoholics (see below). Hence, they are considered by many to be "pre-alcoholics," and should be treated accordingly to forestall that possibility.

<u>Beta:</u> This alcoholic gets sick. He does not become addicted and he suffers no withdrawal symptoms if he stops in tine.

But his poor nutritional habits -- i.e., substituting alcohol for necessary proteins, minerals and vitamins -- lead to such medical complications as peripheral neuritis, cirrhosis of the liver and gastritis. When hospitalized his ailments are all too often treated without regard to the drinking habits that have caused them.

<u>Gamma:</u> These are the alcoholics who most frequently need help from alcoholism clinics and such organizations as Alcoholics Anonymous. Their psychological dependence upon alcohol has grown into a physical dependence. They have lost control over their drinking, and they suffer withdrawal symptoms when they abstain. In early and middle stages of the illness, their tolerance for alcohol is much greater than that of the non-alcoholic. But in late stages their tolerance abruptly decreases to the point where even a single drink can make them ill. (See "Tolerance" and "Progressive Symptoms," below.)

<u>Delta:</u> The Delta alcoholic maintains a steady concentration of alcohol in his bloodstream during his waking hours. Usually he has grown up where alcohol is an all-purpose beverage, served at all meals. But he can be a business executive whose eye openers and three-martinis-for-lunch have become a ritual, or "the little old lady" whose daily quota of dry sherry is a must. Seldom visibly intoxicated, the Delta alcoholic will suffer withdrawal symptoms when forced to abstain. For example, when hospitalized for several days prior to surgery, they may develop delerium tremens.

<u>Epsilon:</u> This is the so called binge drinker, who will go for a long period weeks, months, or even a year without a drink. But once he starts, it is explosive. He continues drinking until he goes into a stupor. If the binges continue with increasing frequency, he may become a Gamma alcoholic.

Dr. Jellinek wrote that there are many other types of alcoholism, more than there are letters in the Greek alphabet. But the above five are the ones the alcoholism counselor is most likely to encounter.

Despite the protests of many alcoholics -- particularly the Gammas, Deltas, and Epsilons -- that they "can take it or leave it" or "only drink on payday," there is one common denominator. Consciously or subconsciously, they are forever looking forward and planning for the next drink, be it tomorrow, next week, or six months from now. This is not conducive to the "comfortable sobriety" that leads to recovery.

V. <u>CAUSES OF ALCOHOLISM</u>

Those engaged in scientific research have yet to establish that there is any hereditary influence in a person's susceptibility to alcohol addiction.

Nor is there any physical basis for alcoholism. However, as already noted, there can be a growing physiological dependence upon alcohol as the disease progresses.

Psychological and personality factors play an important role.

While heredity apparently has no part in determining the possibilities of a youngster's becoming an alcoholic in later years, his environment can. Many surveys indicate that about half the adult alcoholics interviewed have at least one alcoholic parent. Other children may be so repelled by the ugly topsyturvydom of parental drinking that they go through life without touching a drop although they may suffer other emotionally crippling effects.

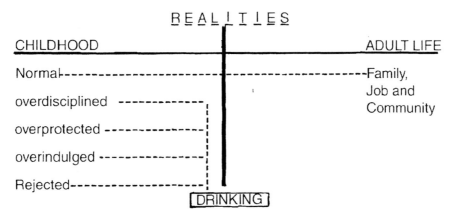

CHILDHOOD EXPERIENCES

More important is the manner in which the child is taught to face reality. As the accompanying "Childhood Experiences" chart indicates, the "normal" child with "normal" parents sees them tackle the problems and decisions in everyday living as they arise. Other things being equal, he will do the same with his lesser difficulties and continue to do so with the big ones in adulthood.

But if the parents overdiscipline, overprotect or overindulge him, he will be more apt to shy away when confronted by any situation that demands his decision or constructive action. Later in life, he discovers that alcohol offers him temporary escape. This discovery eventually leads into habit. As he takes flight in the bottle more and more often, he can develop such a physiological dependency upon it that he is well on the way to full-fledged alcoholism.

The same liability faces the rejected child. Knowing he is not wanted, he is bound to feel a sense of inadequacy. Unless that is overcome, his so called solution to his problems may eventually be the same.

Of course, all alcoholics did not start out in life as overdisciplined, overprotected, overindulged or rejected children. The death of a loved one,

ALCOHOLIC AND NON-ALCOHOLIC TOLERANCE CURVES

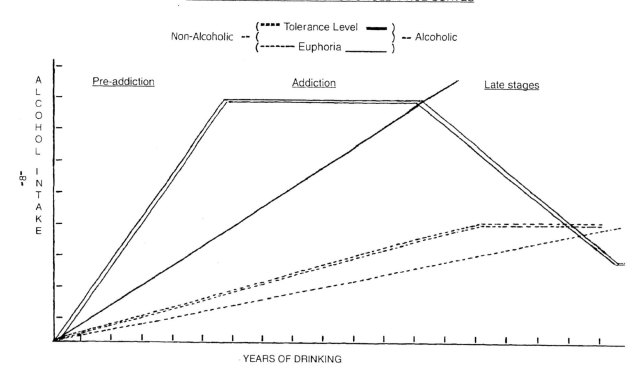

- YEARS OF DRINKING

unavoidable hard times, another's disloyalty, incessant physical pain, etc., can provoke feelings of inadequacy or frustration at any time from the nursery to the grave. When a person repeatedly turns to alcohol as an escape from his anxieties, great or small, he becomes a potential alcoholic.

In short, the onset of alcoholism is not determined by how much a man drinks, but why he drinks.

VI. TOLERANCE

Once embarked, the alcoholic's course is irreversibly charted -- unless he turns to total abstinence at some point along the way. In that case, he can arrest the progress of his illness. He cannot turn back. He cannot retrim his sails for social drinking.

The accompanying diagram of "Alcoholic and Non-Alcoholic Tolerance" indicates the general course the illness takes.

The "alcohol intake" level refers to the amount consumed at any one occasion. As noted above, what is excessive intake for one person is not necessarily excessive for the next. Among other things, it varies according to the physique of the individual.

The "years of drinking" are also relative. The time it takes a novice drinker to become an addict can be anywhere from one to twenty years.

The "euphoria level" is the point at which the drinker reaches Cloud Nine, forgets his inhibitions, and revels in his own fancied charm as well as that of others.

The "tolerance level" is the point at which he gets sick and can drink no more.

Both the alcoholic and non-alcoholic start their drinking histories with one thing in common it takes little alcohol to put them in high spirits and little more to make them sick.

As time passes, both require more alcohol to reach either level. But the alcoholic needs more and more. Because of the greater significance he gives to drinking, during pre-alcoholism years he may learn how to space his drinks and to some extent control his behavior. But he cannot manipulate his tolerance level. That is biologically determined.

There comes the time when the alcoholic's tolerance levels off. This is usually marked by a loss of control -- give him one drink and he is "off to the. races." He has become addicted, physiologically dependent upon alcohol. From this point on, he continues to need more and more to escape everyday reality and regain a sense of euphoria. But his "capacity" before getting sick remains the same. As a result he can handle fewer and fewer drinks after he begins to feel carefree. But he cannot stop in that desirable state of bliss. He is compelled to keep drinking until he is physically unable to drink anymore.

Eventually there comes the day when he drinks just as much, but feels no sense of well-being at all. He only gets sick. (This is the point on the diagram where the tolerance and euphoria lines meet.) Desperately, he goes on benders in search of the alcoholic euphoria he is never to know again. He continues drinking, but gets sick sooner because his tolerance level is plunging down. He discovers that he cannot even keep up with the non-alcoholic friends whom he used to drink under the table any day in the week. One unproductive drink, maybe two, and he is through. His brain and the rest of the body have taken all the alcoholic abuse they can.

VII. PROGRESSIVE SYMPTOMS

The behavioral characteristics of the alcoholic are as progressive as his tolerance to alcohol and the course of the disease itself. They often enable the counselor to determine the relative status of a patient's addiction.

An inventory of some of those symptoms follows. They are not necessarily in precise chronological order. Some may never be experienced by an individual alcoholic. But most of them are experienced and, in toto, are mileposts along the way.

PRE-ADDICTION:

The road to alcoholism begins when drinking is no longer social but a means of psychological escape from the tensions and inhibitions. Although the eventual problem drinker is still in reasonable control, his habits begin to fall into a definite pattern:

1. Gross drinking behavior: He begins to drink more heavily and more often than his friends. "Getting tight" becomes a habit. When drunk, he may develop a "big shot" complex, recklessly spending money, boasting of real and fancied accomplishments, etc.

2. Blackouts: A "blackout," temporary loss of memory, is not to be confused with "pass-out,"

loss of consciousness. The drinker suffering from a blackout cannot remember things he said, things he did, places he visited while carousing the night before or for longer periods. Even a social drinker can have a blackout. With prospective alcoholics, they are more frequent and develop into a pattern.

3. Gulping and sneaking drinks: Anxious to maintain a euphoric level, he begins to toss off drinks at parties and slyly gulp down extra ones when he thinks nobody is looking. He may also "fortify himself" before going to a party to insure his euphoria. He feels guilty about this behavior and skittishly avoids talking about drinks or drinking.

4. Chronic hangovers: As he grows more and more reliant on alcohol as a shock absorber to daily living, "morning after" hangovers become more frequent and increasingly painful. (See "Physiological Effects," above.)

ADDICTION:

Until now the problem drinker has been imbibing heavily but not always conspicuously. More important, he has been able to stop drinking when he so chose. Beyond this point, he develops the symptoms of addiction with increased rapidity:

5. Loss of control: This is the most common symptom that a drinker's pschological habit has become an addiction. He still may refuse to accept a drink. But once he takes a drink, he cannot stop. A single drink is likely to trigger a chain reaction that will continue without a break into a state of complete intoxication.

6. The alibi system: His loss of control induces feelings of guilt and shame. So he concocts an elaborate system of "reasons" for drinking -- "he just completed his income tax," "he failed to complete his income tax," etc. He hopes these will justify his behavior in the eyes of his family and associates. In reality, they are mostly to reassure himself.

7. Eye-openers: He needs a drink in the morning "to start the day right." His morning" may start at any hour of day or night. So an eye-opener is in fact sedation to ease his jangled nerves, hangover, feelings of remorse, etc., after a period of involuntary abstinence, while he was asleep. He cannot face the upcoming hours without alcohol.

8. Changing the pattern: By now he is under pressure from his family, employer, or both. He tries to break the hold alcohol has on him. At first he may try changing brands -- e.g., from whiskey to beer. That docs not good. Then he may set up his own rules on when he will drink and what he will drink -- e.g., only three martinis on weekends and, of course, holidays. He may even "go on the wagon" for a period. Bat one sip of alcohol and the chain reaction starts all over again.

9. Anti-social behavior: He prefers drinking alone or only with other alcoholics, regardless of their social level. He believes that only they can understand him. He broods over imagined wrongs inflicted by others outside this pale and thinks people are staring at him or talking about him. He is highly critical of others and may become violent or destructive.

10. Loss of friends and job: His continuing anti-social behavior causes his friends to avoid him.

The aversion is now mutual. Members of his family may become so helplessly implicated that his wife leaves him "to bring him to his senses." The same situation develops between him, his employer and fellow" workers. And so he loses his job.

11. <u>Seeking medical aid</u>: Physical and mental erosion caused by uncontrolled drinking leads him to make the rounds of hospitals, doctors, psychiatrists, etc. But because he will not admit the extent of his drinking, he seldom receives any lasting benefit. Even when he does halfway "level" with the doctors, he fails to cooperate in following their instructions and the result is the same.

<u>LAST STAGES</u>:

Until he has reached this point, the alcoholic has had a choice: to drink or not to drink that first drink. Once he began, he lost all control. But in the last stages of alcoholism, he has no choice at all. He <u>must</u> drink:

12. <u>Benders</u>: He gets blindly and helplessly drunk for days at a time, hopelessly searching for that feeling of alcoholic euphoria he once appreciated. He utterly disregards everything -- family, job, food, even shelter. These periodic flights into oblivion might be called "drinking to escape the problems caused by drinking."

13. <u>Tremors</u>: In the past his hands may have trembled a bit on "mornings after." But now he gets "the shakes" when he is forced to abstain, a serious nervous condition which racks his whole body. When combined with hallucinations, they are known as the D.T.'s (delerium tremens), often fatal if medical help is not close at hand. During and immediately after an attack, he will swear off liquor forever. He nevertheless comes back for more of the same.

14. <u>Protecting the supply</u>: Having an immediate supply of alcohol available becomes the most important thing in his life to avoid the shakes, if nothing else. He will spend his last cent and, if necessary, sell the coat off his back to get it. Then he hides his bottles so there will always be a drink close at hand when he needs it which can be any hour or minute of day or night.

15. <u>Unreasonable resentments</u>: He shows hostility to others. This can be a conscious effort to protect his precious liquor supply, be it a half-pint on the hip or a dozen quarts secreted about the home. It can also be outward evidence of an unconscious desire to punish himself.

16. <u>Nameless fears and anxieties</u>: He becomes constantly fearful of things he cannot pin down nor describe in words. It is a feeling of impending doom or destruction. This adds to his nervousness and further underscores the compulsion to drink. These fears frequently crop up in the form of hallucinations, both auditory and visual.

17. <u>Collapse of the alibi system</u>: He finally realizes that he can no longer make excuses nor put the blame on others. He has to admit that the fanciful "reasons" he has been fabricating to justify his drinking are preposterous to others and now ridiculous to himself. This may have occurred to him several times during the course of his alcoholic career. But this time it is final. He has to admit that he is licked; that his drinking is beyond his ability to control.

18. <u>Surrender process</u>:   Now if ever, he must give up the idea of ever drinking again and be willing to seek and accept help.

If at this point the alcoholic is unable to surrender, all the signposts point to custodial care or death.

If he has not already suffered extensive and irreversible brain damage, there is a strong likelihood that some form of alcoholic psychosis will develop.

The amnesia and confabulation of Korsakoff's syndrome and the convulsions and comas of Wernicke's disease are possibilities.

Death may come in advanced cases of cirrhosis of the liver, pancreatitis, or hemorrhaging varices of the esophagus.

Or he may arrange his own death by suicide. After all, the suicide rate among alcoholics is three times the normal rate of self-extermination.

VIII. <u>TREATMENT</u>

There is as yet no cure for alcoholism.

The alcoholic is fortunate that the disease is treatable, that it can be arrested. But treatment is of no avail unless that addicted patient subscribes to total abstinence from drinking alcohol in any form. As pointed out above, once he has lost control, he will never regain it.

Also, the sooner the progress of the illness is recognized and arrested, the easier the return to a comfortable and contining sobriety and the less physical and mental deterioration.

The treatment of alcoholism falls into three overlapping lines of action designed for three overlapping objectives:

1. Emergency treatment: Immediate medication, etc., designed to avert physical
disaster or even death.

2. Inpatient treatment: "Drying out." To alleviate the nervous and physical
abnormalities resulting from prolonged and excessive drinking.

3. Follow-up treatment: Psychological rehabilitation necessary for continued sobriety.

Much of the data in the next two sections is for the alcoholism counselor's information only. The prescription and administration of medication and therapeutic procedures are the sole responsibility of authorized medical personnel. However, the counselor should be aware of general practices in order to help the patient and his family arrive at decisions.

A. <u>EMERGENCY TREATMENT</u>

Both acute alcoholic intoxication and many of the withdrawal symptoms which follow can call for prompt treatment in the emergency room of a general hospital.

However, before making a diagnosis of alcohol intoxication, the staff must rule out skull fracture, subdural or subarachnoid hemorrhage, cardio-vascular injury, and diabetic or insulin shock. These are quickly ascertained by laboratory and X-ray tests. Even though blood tests may indicate a high concentration of alcohol in the bloodstream, they do not veto the possibility that other factors may be the primary cause of his condition.

Once alcohol intoxication is diagnosed, it must be remembered that alcohol is in itself a powerful sedative. If the patient is in a stupor or in a comatose state, he should not be given any further sedation.

In cases where treatment for psychomotor agitation (e.g., "the shakes") is indicated, a tranquilizing drug such as Librium is highly effective in reducing tension. Many doctors feel that 100 mgs. given intramuscularly, then followed by smaller amounts taken orally every three or four hours for twelve to twenty-four hours, allow the body to adjust to the abrupt withdrawal of alcohol. Other tran-quilizers such as Thorazine, Sparine, Mellaril, Vistaril, Atarax, etc. are equally effective. An old standby, paraldehyde, has been largely eclipsed by newer drugs because of its habituating properties. Narcotics and barbituates should definitely be avoided because of even more habituating properties. They can only add further addictions to the addiction which already exists.

More serious and sometimes fatal are alcoholic coma, convulsions, hallucinosis and delirium tremens.

Before making a diagnosis of alcoholic coma, the following conditions must be ruled out: skull fracture, subdural or subarachnoid hemorrhage (bleeding in the membranes surrounding the brain), cardio-vascular accident (heart attack), uremia, insulin shock and diabetic coma.

One of the main dangers in alcoholic coma is a respiratory failure, followed by circulatory collapse. It may be necessary to maintain adequate airway to the lungs, use artificial respiration, and/or administer stimulants to the central nervous system. Another danger is the inhalation of vomited matter, which can cause lung abscess or pneumonia. Possible fractures and lacerations resulting from falls must also be considered.

Alcoholic convulsions ("rum fits") closely resemble the grand mal seizures of epilepsy. The examining physician should make certain by electroencephalogram (EEG) if necessary -- that the patient is not suffering from the latter disorder. The primary concern is that he does not injure himself in falling or thrashing about, or by biting or swallowing his tongue, which can cause him to choke to death. A spoon, a leather belt or any device he cannot bite through should be inserted between his teeth. Valium is a useful drug in controlling the attack. To prevent such attacks, Dilantin, an anticonvulsant, is prescribed for alcoholics with a history of seizures.

Alcoholic hallucinosis usually occurs after a patient has been detoxified The hallucinations can be either auditory or visual, with the former more common. They are not as frightening as the fantastic figments encountered during D.T.'s and the patient is usually oriented as to time, place and the existing situation. There is danger of suicide and the patient should be watched.

Delirium tremens (D.T.'s) is a withdrawal symptom which can occur many days after the alcoholic has stopped drinking and, when not immediately treated, can be fatal. As the name implies, it combines visual and auditory hallucinations with extreme tremors and even grand mal type convulsions. Unlike alcoholic hallucinosis, the patient is completely disoriented. His hallucinations take the form of grotesque human and animal ghouls which threaten him from every side. He should be treated in a well lighted room because every shadow can conjure up another evil menace to panic him. An attending nurse, counselor or other aide should not argue about the existence of these phantasms -- only reassure the patient that nobody will harm him. Librium, Vistaril, chlorpromazines and other tranquilizers are used in treatment.

(The gravity of D.T.'s cannot be overemphasied. In a situation where a patient shows signs of impending D.T.'s and no medical help is available, he can be given an ounce or two of whiskey or fortified wine. This will help to stave off the attack until he can be handed over to a hospital emergency room.)

Coma, convulsions, hallucinosis and D.T.'s are definite medical emergencies and should be treated in the hospital until the patient has fully recovered from the immediate crisis.

In other cases of acute phases of chronic alcoholism, if the patient is not too ill he may be discharged in the care of a cooperative family or interested person who will follow medical instructions.

In any event, the patient must be directed to follow up his emergency room treatment by seeing his family doctor, coming back to the hospital's outpatient clinic, or arranging for continued treatment at a public or private alcoholism clinic. This is for his own protection as well as that of the hospital and personnel who attended him.

B. IMPATIENT TREATMENT

Then there are the hundreds, even thousands of non-emergency patients whose prolonged and excessive drinking has left them so mentally and physically "run down" that they are incapable of adequately dealing with their responsibilities at home or on the job. Simply to let them sleep off their drunks or give them tranquilizers to cushion their shakes and then send them on their ways is inviting trouble. Most of then will wander into the nearest tavern or liquor store and promptly find themselves in worse trouble than they were before -- back again in "the revolving door."

What they need is "drying out," both physical and mental. They need to start repairing the damage the persistent drinking has done to their bodies. They need to disentangle their confused thinking before they can even grasp the meaning of any new program of rehabilitation.

For these persons the best solution is six to eight days hospitalization. In this way, constant care and medication is assured. If they suffer withdrawal symptoms -- such as hallucinosis or D.T's -- there is professional help at hand for immediate treatment, or even to avert the attacks. Above all, they are removed from the temptation of sneaking drinks that often undo the good of treatment at home.

Patients are usually kept on bed rest for the first twenty-four hours after admission, during which they are given routine laboratory and X-ray tests. There will be psychomotor agitation as the patient's body adjusts to the abrupt withdrawal of alcohol. Tranquilizers such as Librium, Sparine, Mellaril, Thorazine, Vistaril, or Atarax will keep him in a state of quiet suspense for the first 36 to 48 hours and are gradually tapered off as his condition improves.

At the same time steps are taken to correct the vitamin-mineral deficiency which has been building up over the days, weeks, or months the patient has been drinking instead of eating. He is put on a high protein diet and multivitamins. Orange juice, with a dash of sodium chloride in it, is kept at his bedside. And in cases of severe dehydration, he is given "Philadelphia cocktails" intravenously, which contain a glucose-saline solution, insuline, and vitamins.

As this period of rest and recuperation progresses, his thinking begins to straighten out. This is the time to lay the groundwork for follow-up treatment. He must be made to realize that recovery from chronic alcoholism is not an overnight or eight-day procedure. The damage has been years in the making. Even with his sincere cooperation, it takes one or two years to make basic psychological and physical repairs. This is the time to line him up for continuing treatment at an outpatient clinic, Alcoholics Anonymous, or other therapeutic agencies.

During this period, the patient may also be started on Antabuse (see "Deterrent Therapy," below).

C. FOLLOW-UP TREATMENT

The chronic alcoholic cannot stay sober without help. (One hears of the person who "did it on his own," but one seldom meets him in the flesh.)

The alcoholic needs support. He should have the encouragement of family and friends, if he has any left. But the support of family and friends can be erratic and is not to be found in some areas where he needs help the most.

He constantly needs to remember that he is an alcoholic who cannot afford to take a drink without unfortunate results just as the diabetic cannot afford to forget his ailment and his insulin, or the epileptic his Dilantin.

For years the alcoholic has been committing physical and mental hara-kiri and he may need prolonged medical or psychiatric help.

Alcoholism can be expensive; and, therefore, the patient may be broke. Alcoholism loses jobs; he may need employment. Alcoholism causes dissension; he may seek reconciliation with his family. And so on.

Unless he is spiritually barren, he can be kept reminded of his vulnerability in Alcoholics Anonymous, as well as find understanding and moral support (see below). But if he is in need of professional help and advice in addition to awareness and understanding, an alcoholism clinic is probably his one best resource.

The many roles played by outpatient clinics are described in the next chapter. In brief, their primary concerns are medical and psychiatric services, and individual and group counseling. These are geared to meet the needs of alcoholics at large as well as hospital dischargees.

The medical and psychiatric services can range from consultation and referrals to critical treatment-on-the-spot, depending upon facilities.

The medical and psychiatric services can range from consultation and referrals to critical treatment-on-the-spot, depending upon facilities.

Individual counseling is available to help the patient work out solutions to his very personal problems. This service is hot intended to act as an employment or public welfare resource. But the counselor should be able to refer the patient to appropriate agencies in the community to meet these and other special needs.

Group counseling or "group therapy," to use the term in its broad non-professional sense is the outpatient clinic's major contribution to continued treatment once a patient has emerged from the mental and physical distress of intoxication, and withdrawal.

Continued sobriety can only be achieved by changing the alcoholic's attitude and teaching him new ways of dealing with the frustrations that drove him to drink.

In this type of treatment, the patient is assigned to a small, ongoing group of fellow alcoholics who discuss their common "hang-ups" -- i.e., frustrations and temptations which led to their past drinking -- and what they are doing to meet them without resorting to alcohol. A trained leader -- usually a psychiatrist, psychiatric nurse, social worker or counselor -- merely keeps the discussion within bounds. At first, the new patient is inclined to confine his participation and mental note-taking to alcohol, its use and misuse. As he becomes better acquainted with the other members of the group, he finds himself more and more involved in the discussion of more stressful areas of personal and social functioning. Accordingly, the way is cleared for greater insight into his own personality and behavior and those elements which have contributed to his alcoholism. He is then better able to adapt himself to a more meaningful way of living without recourse to alcohol.

Many psychiatrists feel that group therapy is far more effective than individual psychotherapy. Because of the alcoholic's habit of "sneaking" drinks, protecting his supply, and feelings of guilt, he becomes more and more of a "loner" as his illness progresses. In group treatment he once again becomes physically and psychologically involved with other people. Thus, he is pried loose from the isolation, he has built up for himself not by choice, but because his disease demanded it.

(Both individual and group counseling are more fully discussed in Chapter III.)

D. DETERRENT THERAPY

Disulfiram (Antabuse) is a drug often prescribed to deter the alcoholic from drinking. It is no "cure." It does not erase the desire to drink. But it does make the consequences of drinking the slightest amount of alcohol so agonizing that even the most confirmed dipsomaniac will abstain so long as it remains in his system.

Normally the liver oxidizes alcohol into acetaldehyde which, in turn, breaks down into acetic acid and next into carbon dioxide and water. Acetaldehyde is a poison. Necessary for its breakdown is a enzyme (acetaldehyde dehydrogenase) which the disulfiram blocks. When this happens, the acetaldehyde rapidly accumulates and within a few minutes, the patient becomes violently ill. He becomes extremely hot and flushed. His blood pressure rises rapidly and a splitting headache develops. Concurrently, he develops a pain in the chest which spreads into the left arm, his heart pounds rapidly, and he finds it difficult to breathe. Suddenly, his blood pressure falls and. he may become sick to the stomach and even collapse. He then falls into a deep sleep.

The attack may last up to four hours; but the patient shudders at the thought of experiencing it again.

However, Antabuse has no effect upon the body unless alcohol is taken. It needs a detonator to start the chain reaction. And the only detonator is a drink.

Thus, it acts as or silent policeman to protect the patient's abstinence. The average practicing alcoholic cannot envision life without his favorite beverage to sustain him. Once he starts on an Antabuse regimen, he discovers that sobriety is not only attainable and endurable, but that it can be more agreeable than the way things were with alcohol.

By itself, Antabuse is no panacea to bring about and maintain sobriety. But taken regularly, it acts as a shield against impulsive "slips" which can be serious setbacks in continuing treatment. Once the patient takes his daily dose, he has no decisions to make about drinking or not drinking for the next 72 hours. And it keeps him sober to profit from whatever form of follow-up therapy he may be undergoing.

On the other hand, if a patient who claims that he is "on Antabuse" drinks with no ill effects, the therapist knows that he is not taking his medication as prescribed. It can be reasonably assumed that he has not yet achieved the motivation necessary for any program of recovery.

Because of the reactions that occur when alcohol is taken on top of Antabuse, the patient must have a physical examination before the drug can be prescribed. (Contraindications include uncontrolled hypertension (high blood pressure), coronary heart disease, late stages of cirrhosis, severe pancreatitis, psychoses or brain damage, and sometimes pregnancy.) The patient is given a card to carry with him so he will not be given medication containing alcohol in the event of an emergency. Antabuse should not be administered until 72 hours have elapsed since the patient's last drink; nor should he drink again until at least 72 hours after taking his last pill.

E. MISCELLANEOUS THERAPIES

There are many other types of therapy, most of which the alcoholism counselor will probably never hear about. But there arc several of which he should be aware:

Lysergic acid (LSD) therapy: Research continues on this still unproved method of treatment. Thus far the effectiveness apparently rests in the degree of rapport established between the patient and the individual therapist who attends him on his "trips."

Hypnosis: Used in certain types of psychiatric and psychosomatic illnesses, some practitioners believe hypnosis can be employed in the treatment of alcoholism. Up to now the results have not been very successful.

Conditioned response therapy: The most common of many procedures is to add an emetic to a patient's favorite brand of alcoholic beverage. After several nauseating experiences, he is automatically supposed to develop a distast for the stuff. Chief drawbacks are: (1) that frequent "reconditioning" is necessary; and (2) that patients can often switch to other brands and continue drinking without ill effects.

Psychodrama: This is a form of group therapy wherein the patients act out psychic conflicts. Because of the highly emotional nature of these conflicts, psychodrama should only be employed under the close supervision of a psychiatrist or specially trained psychodrama therapist.

F. ALCOHOLICS ANONYMOUS

Alcoholics Anonymous is a fellowship of problem drinkers who have banded together in an effort to help themselves and other problem drinkers attain sobriety.

Their program is best summed up in "Twelve Steps" which the members are urged to follow:

1. We admitted we were powerless over alcohol -- that our lives had become unmanageable.
2. Cane to believe that a Power greater than ourselves could restore us to sanity.
3. Made a decision to turn our will and our lives over to the care of God as we understood Him.
4. Made a searching and fearless moral inventory of ourselves.
5. Admitted to God, to ourselves, and to another human being the exact nature of our wrongs.
6. Were entirely ready to have God remove all these defects of character.
7. Humbly asked Him to remove our shortcomings.
8. Made a list of all persons we had harmed, and became willing to make amends to them all.
9. Made direct amends to such people wherever possible, except when to do so would injure them or others.
10. Continued to take personal inventory and when we were wrong promptly admitted it.
11. Sought through prayer and meditation to improve our conscious contact with God as we understood Him, praying only for knowledge of His will for us and the power to carry that out.
12. Having had a spiritual awakening as the result of these steps, we tried to carry this message to alcoholics, and to practice these principles in all our affairs.

While "God" is frequently mentioned in these steps, A.A. members are quick to point out that they "adhere to no particular creed or religion" and welcome agnostics into the fellowship. But the spiritual element does play an important role in the "therapy."

Undoubtedly, A.A. has been responsible for many recoveries in the United States and in other countries. This is not surprising in view of its half million members including those not affiliated with any one group and the profusion of those groups, which are to be found in practically any sizable community in the country. With "no dues or fees in A.A.," with no rosters kept (to insure anonymity), with no record of those who may attend one or two meetings and then disappear from sight, it is impossible to estimate the percentage of recoveries. But by the sheer weight of the number of alcoholics exposed, any head-count would be high.

A.A. meetings are either "open" or "closed." Anyone interested in the program, alcoholic or non-alcoholic, can attend the former. Closed meetings are for alcoholics only. They are usually sessions in which the participants discuss more intimate alcoholic experiences. Both meetings are presided over by members chosen on a rotating, week-to-week basis -- i.e., no special training is involved.

One consideration in a sick alcoholic's limiting his treatment to A.A. is the fact that there is no medical or psychiatric screening. A "Twelfth Step worker" enthused over his own improvement, may be apt to disregard an underlying mental or physical disorder that is contributing to the woes of the person who has called for help. But on the whole, A.A. 'ers are becoming increasingly aware of the physiological and psychiatric complications of the disease. More realize that "first things come first" and that physical and mental blocks must be overcome before the ailing alcoholic is ready to comprehend the spiritual.

Many clinic patients regularly attend A.A. meetings, just as many A.A. members find additional support in clinical therapy and Antabuse.

All reliable resources must be used in treating the alcoholic. So the alcoholism counselor should keep schedules of area A.A. meetings on hand at all times. Alcoholics Anonymous has proved its worth.

———

COUNSELING THE ALCOHOLIC

CONTENTS

COUNSELING THE ALCOHOLIC

I.   PHILOSOPHY AND PRINCIPLES

The alcoholic who is not ready to undergo treatment will often protest,. "Only an alcoholic can help an alcoholic!"

That is not true.

But the counselor -- alcoholic or non-alcoholic --who would help the man or woman whose life is disintegrating because of drinking should thoroughly understand the physical and emotional pain involved before attempting to establish rapport.

The essential quality is one of empathy, which the dictionary defines as "the capacity for participating in another's feelings or ideas." It differs from sympathy in that the counselor does not become emotionally involved, allowing the patient's joys and sorrows to affect his own ability to evaluate and advise.

The effective counselor must not only be able to understand others. He must have a real desire to understand others, to explore the whys of human behavior. And he must have an unconditional, positive regard for the individual patient -- a blend of warmth, acceptance, regard, interest, and respect.

He must continually work on his own self-awareness. He should recognize his own hangups and learn to deal with them. One who is able to do this is better able to be a partner in a helping relationship.

He must always remember that he is a counselor, not an analyst nor a judge. Overconcern with personality theories and counseling techniques will endanger rapport, just as premature attempts to arrive at solutions will surely lead to the patient's being shortchanged.

Equipped with a knowledge of the physiological and psychological nature of alcoholism and especially of its progressive symptoms, the trained counselor usually is in a position to assess the general status of the new patient who sits before him. He has a broad idea of the physical pains, emotional distress, and changing attitudes the alcoholic has already suffered. This may be a small start. But it is an important head start in winning acceptance and evolving a program for recovery.

From that point on it is the counselor's job to translate his general observations into full and meaningful particulars about the highly individual person who seeks his help. Once that is accomplished, they can work together towards reasonable decisions and practical steps to be taken.

II.   THREE STAGES OF RELATIONSHIP

Effective relationships between alcoholism counselors and their patients can be broken down into three stages:

The <u>first</u> might be called the subjective period. During this, usually the initial interview, the counselor wins the patient's confidence and establishes his empathy with him. He then gathers as much pertinent information as possible -- e.g., personal data, marriage and family status, employment, hospitalizations and arrests, drinking habits, etc.

The <u>second</u> is an objective stage. The counselor points out to the pa-tient his current status in comparison with known patterns and established facts about the disease. He explains what could lie ahead.

The <u>third</u> stage is one of teamwork. The counselor joins with the patient in building a road to recovery and solving the problems still posed by the past.

III. THE INITIAL INTERVIEW

  A. <u>Importance</u>

The initial interview usually is the most important, not only because "first impressions" tend to linger on, but because it may also be the last.

For a variety of reasons, the counselor may never again set eyes upon his patient. One of the most common -- particularly in outpatient clinics -- is that the patient is not sufficiently motivated to undergo continuing treatment. At the moment, the prospect of a lifetime without drinking is too frightening. He should nevertheless leave the counselor's office knowing that the door will always be open to him, tomorrow or ten years hence.

A sense of security is the key to gaining the new patient's confidence so that he will come back.

So the patient must be satisfied that the counselor will respect whatever confidences he may choose to divulge. He must be reasonably confident that the counselor is not going to berate him as he has been berated in the past. He must be assured that he can lower his defenses and receive understanding instead of recrimination.

The counselor cannot expect to be told pertinent confidences unless the patient has confidence in him.

  B. <u>The Contract</u>
Also in the initial interview, a "contract" should be established.

The patient must be aware that alcoholism is an illness -- not a sin or a sign of weakness of character. Whether or not he is suffering from that illness will be up to him to decide, if he has not   already done so.

If the answer is yes, he has two choices: to accept treatment or to continue drinking. If he chooses the latter, probably, eventually, it will result in custodial care or death.

However, if he sincerely wants to recover, he must accept the fact that he is a sick man who can no longer drink. The counselor and his colleagues cannot do this for him. But they can help him help himself.

Such are the essentials of the initial contract. The counselor can make them clear in any way that best befits the situation or the patient's general attitude at the time. But unless the patient subscribes to them, any recovery program is courting failure.

C.   Eliciting Patient History

The primary concern in a counselor-patient relationship is "Where do we go from here?" But significant facts about the patient's past and present are necessary for any reliable estimate of the situation.

In the course of time, counselors develop their individual methods of eliciting this information. So it would be presumptuous here to advance any hard-and-fast rules about interviewing new patients as one would instruct a student in the operation of a computer. However, there are certain basic principles to be considered.

The truism that "the quality of the answer depends upon the quality of the question" is universally accepted. The patient must be made to feel that he has the interviewer's undivided attention. He can perceive the presence or lack of empathy not only by the questions asked, but also by the counselor's overall manner. The tone of voice can be more persuasive than the questions themselves. Questions that reflect accusation and suspicion on the part of the counselor arouse resentment and suspicion in the patient and can quickly erase whatever rapport has been established in the beginning.

Even the pacing should be adjusted to the patient. Too slow a pace may suggest a difficulty in understanding on the part of the counselor. Too fast a pace can imply lack of interest.

Some questions must of necessity be pointed and direct e.g., date of birth, marital status, employment, etc. Those are to be expected. Other pointed questions - such as those dealing with the patient's parental and childhood background - are more readily answered if the purpose in asking them is explained. But,in general, pithy questions are preferable to those that can be answered yes or no. They can lead to greater insight into the patient's personality.

D.   Problems and Solutions

Then there is the question that slams the door. The patient "clams up." More often than not it touches upon a painful memory which triggers the frigid reaction. It is useless to pursue the point at that time. The counselor can come back to it later in the interview or, as often happens, the patient will inadvertently supply the answer while responding to another evocative question.

In the same category are evasions and obvious lies. Few alcoholics will admit to having more than "a couple of beers" before their accidents, arrests,or other plights. The first meeting is no time to break down their defenses. Usually "the truth will out" -- that the patient had a pint and a half of whiskey between the two beers -- before the interview is over. The counselor should accept both the lie and its disproval without comment. The same holds true for other camouflages thrown up by the patient.

Nor are all answers verbal. The counselor should listen to what the patient does not say, as well as to what he says. The omissions in his explanations and comments are frequently more revealing than the explanations themselves. At the same time, physical clues can also be expressive of the emotional attitude -- e.g., the sweaty palms arising from fear or a sense of guilt, the folded arms of contrariness, the tears of sheer frustration and self-pity.

The most empathic alcoholism counselor in the world could not hope for a perfect batting average among all the applicants who come to him for aid. Perfect rapport cannot be arranged by an admission desk. Sometimes a patient might better be counseled by a worker in the next room or one down the hall. Or he may gravitate to a new group leader, even after weeks of individual counseling by the person who first interviewed him. In such cases, the counselor should have no hesitancy in "letting the patient go."

E. Problems that the Counselor Cannot Solve

The counselor must be able to distinguish between the patients he can help and those he cannot. He should recognize his own capabilities and limitations. It may be that a difficult family or financial situation or some other involved personal problem is causing or substantially contributing to the patient's drinking. When it is apparent that the cause, whatever it may be, is beyond the counselor's ability to help, he should refer the patient to an agency which can.

IV. THE CONTINUING RELATIONSHIP

Most of the above observations also apply to the continuing counselor-patient relationship. Of course, once the ice has been broken in the initial interviews and confidence established, the alcoholic is not apt to revert to lies and evasions with his counselor or physician. If he has normal intelligence, he will have found out that frankness best paves the way for significant planning and decisions.

Nor are there any precise ground rules to guide the counselor in an ongoing relationship. Success lies in adapting himself to the patient's attitude and, through empathy, helping him to plan ways and means of reaching the goals he sincerely wants to reach. In other words, the counselor has to "play it by ear."

A. Basics

But there are several basic "rules of thumb."

In planning ways and means of reaching objectives, final decisions should be made by the patient, not by the counselor.

One must remember that the average alcoholic comes glutted with unasked-for advice -- opinionated guidance supplied by family, parents, employer, best friend, and well-meaning companions. The patient is tired of advice.

So even if the counselor should know the answers, he should forego the role of mastermind. Better he discuss the pros and cons until the patient can view himself and his situation in the cold light of reality and decide for himself what had best be done to remedy matters. This is not to say that the counselor cannot offer alternatives, nor should he allow the patient to decide upon a potentially disastrous course of action. But when the patient himself makes the final decision or believes that he made it -- it becomes a strictly personal matter. It is no longer advice from family, parents, employer, or best friend. It is his own decision and, as such, he has greater confidence in the chances for success, especially with the counselor and his resources to lend support.

B. Constructive Forces

Besides being surfeited with advice, the average alcoholic comes oppressed with feelings of guilt and inferiority and loss of self-respect. The counselor should search out the constructive forces in his client. He must believe in them and their potentialities. And then he must make the patient realize them and believe in them, too. He can always cite the truism that every man is superior to the next man in some respect -- physically, psychologically, or intellectually. Once that asset is recognized, it can become another steppingstone in planning the road to recovery.

One of the beneficial by-products of counseling is catharsis the process by which repressed emotions and memories are brought to consciousness and released. It is an outpouring of emotionally painful thoughts which the patient has been harboring inside himself with perhaps no one available to console or consult, and which he has futile-ly been attempting to drown in drink. The counselor-patient relationship offers an opportunity for such purgative relief.

Catharsis should be fostered, but not forced. As he listens, the counselor should be alert to responses by the patient which reflect feeling rather than mere recollection, emotions rather than intellect. Strongly felt sentiments can reveal themselves at almost any time e.g., while talking about the family's reaction to his drinking, difficulties on the job, strained relation in the community. The bald recital of an occurrence may impulsively be punctuated with the patient's emotional reaction to the event. This is the time for the counselor to encourage him to express his feelings instead of just facts. But his questions and comments should be leading rather than probing, persuasive rather than pressing. Otherwise the patient may crawl back into his private world and slam the door behind him.

V. GROUP COUNSELING

As a general rule alcoholics are more effectively treated in group therapy than in the traditional one-to-one counselor-patient relationship.

This does not mean that the patient's need for individual counseling is completely superseded when he becomes a member of a group. Strictly personal problems may arise. Help from outside resources may be needed. Periods of uncertainty and depression may threaten his new self-command. In such cases, he may need individual counseling for support.

But for ongoing therapy the group affords a climate which the alcoholic has been avoiding for months or even years. Hiding his drinking habits from others or protecting his supply, he has usually become a loner. As participant in a group, he again becomes a member of society a society in miniature, perhaps, but nevertheless, a cooperative body with common aims and interests. It evokes intercommunication and, hopefully, interaction with others so necessary in again facing up to reality and normal living.

This escape from isolation is only one of many benefits a patient can derive from group therapy. The interpersonal relationships with others faced with the same illness gradually reduces his own sensitivity. He finds understanding, reassurance, and support. As time goes on, he gains greater insight into the origins and evolution of his behavior patterns. He is re-educated in ways of adapting himself to reality. And,because the environment is real, not artificial, he can test many of those ways within the group itself.

A. Role of the Group Leader

The group leader -- be he alcoholism counselor, social worker, or psychiatrist -- must always remember that the group belongs to its members. His primary mission is to be a good listener, with any outward participation kept to a minimum. The members must feel that they are the ones who are choosing the questions for discussion, arriving at the answers,settling any conflicts or confrontations.

However passive his role may appear to be, the leader must see to it that the discussion does not wander too far away from the subject. He should encourage participation by the silent minority, if any. He should act to relieve tensions and mediate debates. And, at all times, he should be noting the actions and reactions of the individual members, for these are clues to their progress in the recovery program.

While all these duties might seem to conflict with the leader's role as passive observer, he can usually delegate action to others.

Every group is made up of as many different personalities as there are members. They unconsciouly tend to assume various roles which they continue to play week after week. The leader can usually count upon them to function as needed. Among them are: The

Initiator--introduces new ideas or subjects for discussion.
Information-seeker -- asks for pertinent facts.
Information-giver, -- always ready to supply those pertinent facts if he can.
Elaborator -- develops others' comments and ideas.
Orienter -- raises questions about the direction of discussion.
Coordinator -- tries to pull ideas and suggestions together.
Tester -- checks whether the group is ready for decision.
Opinion-giver -- states what he believes to be the consensus of the group.
Such members -- and other members in other roles -- are the group leader's advocates.

B. Measuring the Success of the Group

Superficially, it might seem easiest to measure the success of any group by the faithful attendance of its members and its attraction of new members.

But the true effectiveness of a group is best reflected in its contribution to its members' recovery. From time to time, the leader should ask himself these questions:

Has our group created an atmosphere in which constructive progress can be made?

Has it achieved real communication among members?

Do the members freely give and freely receive help?

Are the conditions such that each member can make his own special contribution?

Does it allow conflict and confrontation to be resolved into creative problem solving?

Has it evolved acceptable ways of making decisions?

If the leader can answer yes to all of these questions, he and the group are accomplishing their mission. If not, he had better diagnose the shortcomings and repair them.

VI. GROUP THERAPY AND A.A.

One frequently hears Alcoholics Anonymous vaguely referred to as "group psychotherapy."

In reality, there are many basic differences between the two methods of treatment. But a layman's misunderstanding can be forgiven since both have one aim among others -- to help the alcoholic stop drinking.

The counselor should be aware of these differences because the confusion is a common one.

A. Differences Between   the Two Methods

In balancing method, it is best to disregard A.A.'s open meetings, where the general public is invited to attend, and limit comparisons to A.A.'s closed meetings, for alcoholics only.

Both A.A. and clinical groups are open to all alcoholics regardless of race, sex, or socio-economic status. While the latter are deliberately kept heterogeneous, members of A.A. tend to gravitate to groups composed of racial and socio-economic peers.

Both stress confidentiality. Outside visitors are not allowed. A.A. closed meetings do not permit the non-alcoholic spouses of members to attend. Clinical groups,recognizing alcoholism as a family disease, urge participation by members' families.

So long as alcoholic patients are under clinical treatment, they are required to attend group meetings, which are usually limited in size -- preferably six to nine participants. A.A. members are not required to attend meetings. Nor are there any limitations as to size. Hence, the same group can vary greatly from week to week in both numbers and make-up.

Leadership in clinical groups is vested in a trained psychotherapist or alcoholism counselor who unobtrusively steers discussion, mediates differences, and, when called upon, answers pertinent questions concerning alcohol and alcoholism. A.A. groups are presided over by a chairman, usually selected weekly on a rotating basis. The only requirement is to be an abstaining alcoholic.

The cornerstone of A.A. therapy is belief in a "God as one understands Him" and reliance upon His power to effect "a spiritual awakening" which will support a new, continuing life without alcohol. Catharsis and reparation for past wrongs committed against others are intended to alleviate guilt. Identification with other members who have succeeded in the program is stressed. Abstinence is the goal.

Clinical therapy, on the other hand, centers on psychological aspects. The alcoholic's nonrational and fantastic life theme is brought out and, through inter-communication and interaction with other group members, is eventually accepted by the patient and hopefully altered. The strengthening of relationships with other group members develops a sense of responsibility both for himself and for others. Full sobriety, not merely abstinence, is the goal.

In A.A., life membership is encouraged for continuing support. In clinical therapy, the successful member eventually leaves the group and stands on his own.

There are other differences, but these are the basic ones. The two therapies do not contravene one another. For many patients, they complement each other. When such is the case, the alcoholic can profitably embrace both.

PSYCHIATRIC NURSING GUIDE
ALCOHOLISM

CONTENTS

———

PSYCHIATRIC NURSING GUIDE
ALCOHOLISM

I. BEHAVIOR

A. Early clues. Drinking excessively when one does not mean to; drinking first thing in morning, missing time from work, especially Monday; repeatedly asks physician for excuses from work "for stomach aches" or "colds"; frequent drinking sprees; blackouts; drinking alone; drinking for real or imagined illness; irritable, fatigued; appetite and weight loss; insomnia; repeated accidents on or off the job; decreasing or erratic performance.

B. Patient characteristics and symptoms. Shakiness, jitteriness, weakness; insecure and resentful toward self, family, professional people, church (authority figures especially); hostile, demanding, rebellious and critical; inadequate, inferior, self-piteous, depressed, guilty, helpless and hopeless; lonely and isolated; lacks self respect; often perfectionistic and intolerant of self and others; fearful, distrustful and somewhat paranoid; often denies, minimizes and/or rationalizes drinking; low tolerance for pain (emotional and physical) and frustration; frequently overindulgent in other areas of oral satisfaction (smoking, eating, medication, etc.); feels unloved and worthless; often has a likable and charming personality, though a somewhat superior facade. Usually does not wear well and frequently attempts to manipulate situations and people; uncanny ability to bend regulations, split staff relations and induce hostility in staff; adept at maneuvering significant person into position of being "guilty" or causative party for his drinking; makes rules, then changes them to suit his purpose; bends reality.

C. Impending delirium tremens. Restlessness, agitation, inability to relax and sleep.

II. LONG TERM GOALS

A. to help patient to accept the fact:
1. That at least some of his difficulties are a result of drinking;
2. That alcoholism is an illness of and in itself; and
3. That his life must be managed without alcohol.

B. To help patient:
1. To find methods of therapeutic substitutes to supply the needs that alcohol supplied, and
2. To regain his self-respect and confidence.

C. To bring patient hope of arresting alcoholism.

III. SHORT TERM GOALS

A. To help him to learn:
1. That satisfaction and support can be obtained from relating to others, individually as well as in groups.
2. Alternate acceptable methods of relieving tension and anxiety.

B. To help him:
1. Tolerate frustration.
2. Identify ways of preventing or alleviating feelings of loneliness.
3. Gain confidence by working with his hands and successfully completing a project.

C. To control symptoms of impending delirium tremens.

IV. APPROACH

A. Acute withdrawal and impending delirium tremens
  ❖ Provide protective supervision to prevent injury if patient is confused or disoriented (one-to-one, reduce sound).
  ❖ Observe for symptoms of impending delirium tremens and/or convulsions. Provide a quiet atmosphere that is well lighted, if extremely tremulous.
  ❖ Avoid sudden abrupt approaches that may excite.
  ❖ Encourage fluid intake, especially sweetened fruit juices, unless contraindicated, until he is able to eat solids.
  ❖ Use measures to induce sleep and rest (control noise, light, warm shower at night, hot drink). Get him to sleep promptly and keep him asleep as long as possible.
  ❖ Give drugs as ordered to keep patient well sedated during withdrawal (med. order).
  ❖ Observe for maintenance of vital signs.
  ❖ Do not permit out of bed alone during withdrawal or highly sedated periods.
  ❖ Force fluids when dehydrated (water, fruit juices, ginger ale, other).
  ❖ Keep accurate records of intake/output during detoxification period.
  ❖ Encourage patient to eat a high protein diet and to take supplementary vitamins, feed if necessary while highly sedated.
  ❖ Explain reasons for all tests.
  ❖ Let patient talk about his problems while waiting for drugs to take effect.
  ❖ Draw out his feelings of resentment, hopelessness, guilt and remorse, as well as rationalizations and alibis.
  ❖ Encourage snacking at all hours.
  ❖ Use decaffeinated coffee.

B. Continuing Treatment
  ❖ Accept alcoholism for what it actually is: a disease which even if it cannot be cured, can be permanently arrested.
  ❖ Plan regular routines that provide an adequate amount of rest, work, socialization and interaction with others.
  ❖ Observe for symptoms of depression.
  ❖ Encourage him to make decisions for himself, provided they are within the limits set by hospital and unit policies
  ❖ Confront patient with his manipulation.
  ❖ Insist he complete a project or work assignment that is started.
  ❖ Be firm, helpful, understanding.
  ❖ Listen calmly when he ventilates anger and hostility.
  ❖ Encourage participation in and responsibility for recreational activities, especially nonspectator type.
  ❖ Avoid being caught in the "trap" of his maneuvering one person against another.
  ❖ Give emotional support through sincere interest and attention without becoming overly sympathetic.
  ❖ Avoid reinforcement of patient's feelings of shame and unworthiness.
  ❖ Do not accept at face value the patient's explanation and reassurances while minimizing his drinking or boasting about escapades. (Show disinterest to boasting about episodes.)
  ❖ Assist him to tone down his superior attitude.
  ❖ Promote patient's talents and assets in group activities with other patients as well as personnel.
  ❖ When unreasonable demands are made, use a firm approach with kindness in a calm, matter-of-fact manner.
  ❖ Spend time with patient when he begins to improve to allay loneliness.

- ❖ Provide diversion for the convalescent patient.
- ❖ Introduce patient to outpatient service while he is still hospitalized.
- ❖ Accept admission of alcoholism as a problem with kindness and nonjudgment.
- ❖ Welcome a patient at any time, intoxicated or sober, regardless of the number of slips.
- ❖ Build ego strength when he expresses remorse, e.g., "What are you going to do to keep this from happening again?" "How would you handle yourself in a similar situation?"
- ❖ Refer patient to Alcoholics Anonymous.
- ❖ Attend open AA meetings.
- ❖ Persuade patient he is worth saving.
- ❖ Accept patient without reservation which will make him worthy of your concern.
- ❖ Accept the alcoholic as worthy of your best effort.
- ❖ Keep calm.
- ❖ Point out to a patient with severe medical problems that drinking might aggravate his condition.
- ❖ Provide a permissive climate.
- ❖ Recognize that the alcoholic dislikes authority, rules, and regulations.
- ❖ Establish yourself as a nonjudgmental listening post.
- ❖ Encourage patient to care for own needs.
- ❖ Delegate responsibility for keeping appointments, attending to personal hygiene, getting to meals, and doing own housekeeping.
- ❖ Encourage patient to help other patients.
- ❖ Provide meetings where complaints and gripes are aired, ward policies are drawn up and acted upon, and great efforts are made toward reaching unanimous agreement on policies among patients and staff.
- ❖ Allow patient to plan for social functions.
- ❖ Accompany patients to social activities.
- ❖ Refer patient and family to other community resources for help with alcoholism.

V. CONCEPTS/PRINCIPLES

- ❖ Physical rehabilitation and a nutritional regime are necessary for the restoration of physical stamina because alcoholism ruins a person physically.
- ❖ The treatment and nursing care of the alcoholic patient begins with understanding his personality and the problems from which he has a need to escape.
- ❖ The primary treatment of the alcoholic is to aid him in meeting life's responsibilities without using alcohol as an escape mechanism.
- ❖ The permanent rehabilitation of the alcoholic patient is largely influenced by his personal motivation to give up his emotional crutch.
- ❖ The problem of alcoholism is thought to have its basis in some emotional conflict, frustration, or overwhelming feeling of inadequacy.
- ❖ The treatment of the alcoholic cannot be accomplished by rejection from personnel.
- ❖ The alcoholic is skilled at building self-esteem of personnel in order to obtain favors, or to have staff overlook minor infractions of ward policies.
- ❖ The alcoholic often takes a reality premise and bends or stretches the situation which evokes feelings of embarrassment or animosity in a person he has picked as his "Patsy".
- ❖ Many alcoholics have self-destructive tendencies and seek in their drinking a kind of oblivion that helps them to escape from the realities they find intolerable and with which they cannot cope.
- ❖ The difference between the social drinker and the alcoholic lies in control.
- ❖ Some cases of alcoholism are the result of mental illness in which the drinking is an overlay of the underlying condition.
- ❖ Alcoholism is no respector of sex, nationality, or social status.

❖ The person with alcoholism has a compulsion, possibly based on a physiochemical reaction, to continue drinking once he has started.

❖ The only time the alcoholic has any real control over his drinking is in his choice of whether or not to take the first drink.

❖ Alcoholism requires intelligent medical treatment and can be successfully managed.

❖ The person who has had enough difficulty (with his family, social life, job, law enforcement, or physical symptoms) to seek help, merits help.

❖ Acceptance of a way of life without alcohol usually does not take place the first time a patient is confronted with his alcoholism.

❖ Relapses are often a necessary part of the patient's education; each one reminds him again and again that the only course for him is continuing abstinence.

❖ The alcoholic must never be considered cured. He must have medical care for the rest of his life.

❖ During recovery from the acute phase, the patient's usual defenses are vulnerable and he is more readily influenced.

❖ The alcoholic has deep unsatisfied longings for love, power, and prestige which he knows he has little chance of ever fulfilling.

VI. PROBLEMS WHICH PREVENT REACHING GOALS

❖ Critical and rejecting attitude of personnel regarding alcoholism.

❖ Lack of motivation on patient's part to give up drinking (e.g., refusing to admit he has a problem with alcohol).

❖ Failure to confront patient with his manipulating behavior.

❖ Feeling guilty when patient adeptly shifts responsibility for his problem to someone else.

❖ Many a patient has resisted treatment because of the supercilious or condescending attitude of those supposedly attempting to help him.

❖ False belief of alcoholic patient that staff is "against him" rather than "for him".

❖ Many of the staff starts out with the same moral, disdainful attitude that the general public has toward alcohol.

❖ Being barely tolerant, showing annoyance and being curt and hurried.

❖ Resenting intrusion on time when patient begins to feel better.

————

DRUG ABUSE

CONTENTS

DRUG ABUSE
CONTROLLED SUBSTANCES ACT

The Controlled Substances Act (CSA), Title II of the Comprehensive Drug Abuse Prevention and Control Act of 1970, is the legal foundation of the government's fight against abuse of drugs and other substances. This law is a consolidation of numerous laws regulating the manufacture and distribution of narcotics, stimulants, depressants, hallucinogens, anabolic steroids and chemicals used in the illicit production of controlled substances.

CONTROLLING DRUGS OR OTHER SUBSTANCES

FORMAL SCHEDULING

The CSA places all substances which were in some manner regulated under existing Federal law into one of five schedules. This placement is based upon the substance's medical use, potential for abuse, and safety or dependence liability. The Act also provides a mechanism for substances to be controlled, or added to a schedule; decontrolled, or removed from control; and rescheduled or transferred from one schedule to another. The procedure for these actions is found in Section 201 of the Act (21 D.S.C. 811).

Proceedings to add, delete, or change the schedule of a drug or other substance may be initiated by the Drug Enforcement Administration (DEA), the Department of Health and Human Services (HHS), or by petition from any interested party: the manufacturer of a drug, a medical society or association, a pharmacy association, a public interest group concerned with drug abuse, a state or local government agency, or an individual citizen. When a petition is received by DEA, the agency begins its own investigation of the drug.

The agency also may begin an investigation of a drug at any time based upon information received from law enforcement laboratories, state and local law enforcement and regulatory agencies, or other sources of information.

Once DEA has collected the necessary data, the Administrator of DEA, by authority of the Attorney General, requests from HHS a scientific and medical evaluation and recommendation as to whether the drug or other substance should be controlled or removed from control. This request is sent to the Assistant Secretary of Health of HHS. HHS solicits information from the Commissioner of the Food and Drug Administration (FDA), evaluations and recommendations from the National Institute on Drug Abuse, and on occasion from the scientific and medical community at large. The Assistant Secretary, by authority of the Secretary, compiles the information and transmits back to DEA a medical and scientific evaluation regarding the drug or other substance, a recommendation as to whether the drug should be controlled, and in what schedule it should be placed.

The medical and scientific evaluations are binding on DEA with respect to scientific and medical matters. The recommendation on scheduling is binding only to the extent that if HHS recommends that the substance not be controlled, DEA may not control the substance.

Once DEA has received the scientific and medical evaluation from HHS, the Administrator will evaluate all available data and make a final decision whether to propose that a drug or other substance should be controlled and into which schedule it should be placed.

The threshold issue is whether the drug or other substance has potential for abuse. If a drug does not have a potential for abuse, it cannot be controlled. Although the term "potential for abuse" is not defined in the CSA, there is much discussion of the term in the legislative history of the Act. The following items are indicators that a drug or other substance has a potential for abuse:

1) There is evidence that individuals are taking the drug or other substance in amounts sufficient to create a hazard to their health or to the safety of other individuals or to the community; or

2) There is significant diversion of the drug or other substance from legitimate drug channels; or

3) Individuals are taking the drug or other substance on their own initiative rather than on the basis of medical advice from a practitioner licensed by law to administer such drugs; or

4) The drug is a new drug so related in its action to a drug or other substance already listed as having a potential for abuse to make it likely that the drug will have the same potential for abuse as such drugs, thus making it reasonable to assume that there may be significant diversions from legitimate channels, significant use contrary to or without medical advice, or that it has a substantial capability of creating hazards to the health of the user or to the safety of the community. Of course, evidence of actual abuse of a substance is indicative that a drug has a potential for abuse.

In determining into which schedule a drug or other substance should be placed, or whether a substance should be decontrolled or rescheduled, certain factors are required to be considered. Specific findings are not required for each factor. These factors are listed in Section 201 (c), [21 U.S.C. 811 (c)], of the CSA and are as follows:

1) *The drug's actual or relative potential for abuse.*

2) *Scientific evidence of the drug's pharmacological effects.* The state of know 1edge with respect to the effects of a specific drug is, of course, a major consideration. For example, it is vital to know whether or not a drug has a hallucinogenic effect if it is to be controlled because of that. The best available knowledge of the pharmacological properties of a drug should be considered.

3) *The state of current scientific knowledge regarding the substance.* Criteria (2) and (3) are closely related. However, (2) is primarily concerned with pharmacological effects and (3) deals with all scientific knowledge with respect to the substance.

4) *Its history and current pattern of abuse.* To determine whether or not a drug should be controlled, it is important to know the pattern of abuse of that substance, including the socio-economic characteristics of the segments of the population involved in such abuse.

5) *The scope, duration, and significance of abuse.* In evaluating existing abuse, the Administrator must know not only the pattern of abuse but whether the abuse is widespread. In reaching his decision, the Administrator should consider the economics of regulation and enforcement attendant to such a decision. In addition, he should be aware of the social significance and impact of such a decision upon those people, especially the young that would be affected by it.

6) *What, if any, risk there is to the public health.* If a drug creates dangers to the public health, in addition to or because of its abuse potential, then these dangers must also be considered by the Administrator.

7) *The drug's psychic or physiological dependence liability.* There must be an assessment of the extent to which a drug is physically addictive or psychologically habit-forming, if such information is known.

8) *Whether the substance is an immediate precursor of a substance already controlled.* The CSA allows inclusion of immediate precursors on this basis alone into the appropriate schedule and thus safeguards against possibilities of clandestine manufacture.

After considering the above listed factors, the Administrator must make specific findings concerning the drug or other substance. This will determine into which schedule the drug or other substance will be placed. These schedules are established by the CSA. They are as follows:

Schedule I

- ➤ The drug or other substance has a high potential for abuse.
- ➤ The drug or other substance has no currently accepted medical use in treatment in the United States.
- ➤ There is a lack of accepted safety for use of the drug or other substance under medical supervision.
- ➤ Some Schedule I substances are heroin, LSD, marijuana, and methamphetamine

Schedule II

- ➤ The drug or other substance has a high potential for abuse.
- ➤ The drug or other substance has a currently accepted medical use in treatment in the United States or a currently accepted medical use with severe restrictions.
- ➤ Abuse of the drug or other substance may lead to severe psychological or physical dependence.
- ➤ Schedule II substances include morphine, PCP, cocaine, methadone, and methamphetamine.

Schedule III

- ➤ The drug or other substance has a potential for abuse less than the drugs or other substances in Schedules I and II.
- ➤ The drug or other substance has a currently accepted medical use in treatment in the United States.
- ➤ Abuse of the drug or other substance may lead to moderate or low physical dependence or high psychological dependence.
- ➤ Anabolic steroids, codeine and hydrocodone with aspirin or Tylenol®, and some barbiturates are Schedule III substances.

Schedule IV

- ➤ The drug or other substance has a low potential for abuse relative to the drugs or other substances in Schedule III.
- ➤ The drug or other substance has a currently accepted medical use in treatment in the United States.
- ➤ Abuse of the drug or other substance may lead to limited physical dependence or psychological dependence relative to the drugs or other substances in Schedule III.
- ➤ Included in Schedule IV are Darvon®, Talwin®, Equanil®, Valium® and Xanax®.

Schedule V

> ➤ The drug or other substance has a low potential for abuse relative to the drugs or other substances in Schedule IV.
> ➤ The drug or other substance has a currently accepted medical use in treatment in the United States.
> ➤ Abuse of the drug or other substances may lead to limited physical dependence or psychological dependence relative to the drugs or other substances in Schedule IV.
> ➤ Over-the-counter cough medicines with codeine are classified in Schedule V.

When the Administrator of DEA has determined that a drug or other substance should be controlled, decontrolled, or rescheduled, a proposal to take action is published in the F federal Register. The proposal invites all interested persons to file comments with DEA. Affected parties may also request a hearing with DEA. If no hearing is requested, DEA will evaluate all comments received and publish a final order in the Federal Register, controlling the drug as proposed or with modifications based upon the written comments filed. This order will set the effective dates for imposing the various requirements imposed under the CSA.

If a hearing is requested, DEA will enter into discussions with the party or parties requesting a hearing in an attempt to narrow the issue for litigation. If necessary, a hearing will then be held before an Administrative Law Judge. The judge will take evidence on factual issues and hear arguments on legal questions regarding the control of the drug. Depending on the scope and complexity of the issues, the hearing may be brief or quite extensive. The Administrative Law Judge, at the close of the hearing, prepares findings of fact and conclusions of law and a recommended decision which is submitted to the Administrator of DEA. The Administrator will review these documents, as well as the underlying material, and prepare his/her own findings of fact and conclusions of law (which may or may not be the same as those drafted by the Administrative Law Judge). The Administrator then publishes a final order in the Federal Register either scheduling the drug or other substance or declining to do so.

Once the final order is published in the *Federal Register*, interested parties have 30 days to appeal to a U.S. Court of Appeals to challenge the order. Findings of fact by the Administrator are deemed conclusive if supported by "substantial evidence." The order imposing controls is not stayed during the appeal, however, unless so ordered by the Court.

Emergency or Temporary Scheduling

The CSA was amended by the Comprehensive Crime Control Act of 1984. This Act included a provision which allows the Administrator of DE A to place a substance, on a temporary basis, into Schedule I when necessary to avoid an imminent hazard to the public safety.

This emergency scheduling authority permits the scheduling of a substance which is not currently controlled, is being abused, and is a risk to the public health while the formal rule making procedures described in the CSA are being conducted. This emergency scheduling applies only to substances with no accepted medical use. A temporary scheduling order may be issued for one year with a possible extension of up to six months if formal scheduling procedures have been initiated. The proposal and order are published in the Federal Register as are the proposals and orders for formal scheduling. [21 V.S.C. 811 (1)]

Controlled Substance Analogues

A new class of substances was created by the Anti-Drug Abuse Act of 1986. Controlled substance analogues are substances which are not controlled substances, but may be found in the illicit traffic. They are structurally or pharmacologically similar to Schedule I or II controlled substances and have no legitimate medical use. A substance which meets the definition of a controlled substance analogue and is intended for human consumption is treated under the CSA as if it were a controlled substance in Schedule I.

International Treaty Obligations

U. S. treaty obligations may require that a drug or other substance be controlled under the CSA, or rescheduled if existing controls are less stringent than those required by a treaty. The procedures for these scheduling actions are found in Section 201 (d) of the Act. [21 V.S.C. 811 (d)]

The United States is a party to the Single Convention on Narcotic Drugs of 1961, designed to establish effective control over international and domestic traffic in narcotics, coca leaf, cocaine, and cannabis. A second treaty, the Convention on Psychotropic Sub- stances of 1971, which entered into force in 1976, is designed to establish comparable control over stimulants, depressants, and hallucinogens. Congress ratified this treaty in 1980.

II. REGULATION

The CSA creates a closed system of distribution for those authorized to handle controlled substances. The cornerstone of this system is the registration of all those authorized by DEA to handle controlled substances. All individuals and firms that are registered are required to maintain complete and accurate inventories and records of all transactions involving controlled substances, as well as security for the storage of controlled substances.

Registration

Any person who handles or intends to handle controlled substances must obtain a registration issued by DEA. A unique number is assigned to each legitimate handler of controlled drugs: importer, exporter, manufacturer, distributor, hospital, pharmacy, practitioner, and researcher. This number must be made available to the supplier by the customer prior to the purchase of a controlled substance. Thus, the opportunity for unauthorized transactions is greatly diminished.

Recordkeeping

The CSA requires that complete and accurate records be kept of all quantities of controlled substances manufactured, purchased, and sold. Each substance must be inventoried every two years. Some limited exceptions to the recordkeeping requirements may apply to certain categories of registrants.

From these records it is possible to trace the flow of any drug from the time it is first imported or manufactured through the distribution level, to the pharmacy or hospital that dispensed it, and then to the actual patient who received the drug. The mere existence of this requirement is sufficient to discourage many forms of diversion. It actually serves large drug corporations as an internal check to uncover diversion, such as pilferage by employees.

There is one distinction between scheduled items for recordkeeping requirements. Records for Schedule I and II drugs must be kept separate from all other records of the handler; records for Schedule III, IV, and V substances must be kept in a "readily retrievable" form. The former method allows for more expeditious investigations involving the highly abusable substances in Schedules I and II.

Distribution

The keeping of records is required for distribution of a controlled substance from one manufacturer to another, from manufacturer to distributor, and from distributor to dispenser. In the case of Schedule I and II drugs, the supplier must have a special order form from the customer. This order form (DEA Form 222) is issued by DEA only to persons who are properly registered to handle Schedules I and II. The form is preprinted with the name and address of the customer. The drugs must be shipped to this name and address. The use of this device is a special reinforcement of the registration requirement; it makes doubly certain that only authorized individuals may obtain Schedule I and II drugs. Another benefit of the form is the special monitoring it permits. The form is issued in triplicate: the customer keeps one copy; two copies go to the supplier who, after filling the order, keeps a copy and forwards the third copy to the nearest DEA office.

For drugs in Schedules III, IV, and V, no order form is necessary. The supplier in each case, however, is under an obligation to verify the authenticity of the customer. The supplier is held fully accountable for any drugs which are shipped to a purchaser who does not have a valid registration.

Manufacturers must submit periodic reports of the Schedule I and II controlled substances they produce in bulk and dosage forms. They also report the manufactured quantity and form of each narcotic substance listed in Schedules III, IV, and V, as well as the quantity of synthesized psychotropic substances listed in Schedules I, II, III, and IV. Distributors of controlled substances must report the quantity and form of all their transactions of controlled drugs listed in Schedules I and II and narcotics listed in Schedule III. Both manufacturers and distributors are required to provide reports of their annual inventories of these controlled substances. This data is entered into a system called the Automated Reports and Consolidated Orders System (ARCOS). It enables DEA to monitor the distribution of controlled substances throughout the country, and to identify retail level registrants that receive unusual quantities of controlled substances.

Dispensing to Patients

The dispensing of a controlled substance is the delivery of the controlled substance to the ultimate user, who may be a patient or research subject. Special control mechanisms operate here as well. Schedule I drugs are those which have no currently accepted medical use in the United States; they may, therefore, be used in the United States only in research situations. They generally are supplied by only a limited number of firms to properly registered and qualified researchers. Controlled substances may be dispensed by a practitioner by direct administration, by prescription, or by dispensing from office supplies. Records must be maintained by the practitioner of all dispensing of controlled substances from office supplies and of certain administrations. The CSA does not require the practitioner to maintain copies of prescriptions, but certain states require the use of multiple copy prescriptions for Schedule II and other specified controlled substances.

The determination to place drugs on prescription is within the jurisdiction of the FDA. Unlike other prescription drugs, however, controlled substances are subject to additional restrictions. Schedule II prescription orders must be written and signed by the practitioner; they may not be telephoned into the pharmacy except in an emergency. In addition, a prescription for a Schedule II drug may not be refilled; the patient must see the practitioner again in order to obtain more drugs. For Schedule III and IV drugs, the prescription order may be either written or oral (that is, by telephone to the pharmacy). In addition, the patient may (if authorized by the practitioner) have the prescription refilled up to five times and at any time within six months from the date of the initial dispensing.

Schedule V includes some prescription drugs and many over-the-counter narcotic preparations, including antitussives and antidiarrheal. Even here, however, the law imposes restrictions beyond those normally required for the over-the-counter sales; for example, the patient must be at least 18 years of age, must offer some form of identification, and have his or her name entered into a special log maintained by the pharmacist as part of a special record.

Quotas

DEA limits the quantity of Schedule I and II controlled substances which may be produced in the United States in any given calendar year. By utilizing available data on sales and inventories of these controlled substances, and taking into account estimates of drug usage provided by the FDA, DEA establishes annual aggregate production quotas for Schedule I and II controlled substances. The aggregate production quota is allocated among the various manufacturers who are registered to manufacture the specific drug. DEA also allocates the amount of bulk drug which may be procured by those companies which prepare the drug into dosage units.

Security

DEA registrants are required by regulation to maintain certain security for the storage and distribution of controlled substances. Manufacturers and distributors of Schedule I and II substances must store controlled substances in specially constructed vaults or highly rated safes, and maintain electronic security for all storage areas. Lesser physical security requirements apply to retail level registrants such as hospitals and pharmacies.

All registrants are required to make every effort to ensure that controlled substances in their possession are not diverted into the illicit market. This requires operational as well as physical security. For example, registrants are responsible for ensuring that controlled substances are distributed only to other registrants that are authorized to receive them or to legitimate patients and consumers.

III. PENALTIES

The CSA provides penalties for unlawful manufacturing, distribution, and dispensing of controlled substances. The penalties are basically determined by the schedule of the drug or other substance, and sometimes are specified by drug name, as in the case of marijuana. As the statute has been amended since its initial passage in 1970, the penalties have been altered by Congress. The charts on pages 8 and 9 are an overview of the penalties for trafficking or unlawful distribution of controlled substances. This is not inclusive of the penalties provided under the CSA.

User Accountability/Personal Use Penalties

On November 19, 1988, Congress passed the Anti-Drug Abuse Act of 1988, P. L. 100690. Two sections of this Act represent the Federal Government's attempt to reduce drug abuse by dealing not just with the person who sells the illegal drug, but also with the person who buys it. The first new section is titled "User Accountability" and is codified at 21 U.S.C. § 862 and various sections of Title 42, U.S.C. The second involves "personal use amounts" of illegal drugs, and is codified at 21 U.S.C. § 844a.

User Accountability

The purpose of User Accountability is to not only make the public aware of the Federal Government's position on drug abuse, but to describe new programs intended to decrease drug abuse by holding drug abusers personally responsible for their illegal activities, and imposing civil penalties on those who violate drug laws.

It is important to remember that these penalties are in addition to the criminal penalties drug abusers are already given, and do not replace those criminal penalties.

The new User Accountability programs call for more instruction in schools, kindergarten through senior high, to educate children on the dangers of drug abuse. These programs will include participation by students, parents, teachers, local businesses and the local, state and Federal Government.

User Accountability also targets businesses interested in doing business with the Federal Government. This program requires those businesses to maintain a drug free workplace, principally through educating employees on the dangers of drug abuse, and by informing employees of the penalties they face if they engage in illegal drug activity on company property.

There is also a provision in the law that makes public housing projects drug-free by evicting those residents who allow their units to be used for illegal drug activity, and denies Federal benefits, such as housing assistance and student loans, to individuals convicted of illegal drug activity. Depending on the offense, an individual may be prohibited from ever receiving any benefit provided by the Federal Government.

Personal Use Amounts

This section of the 1988 Act allows the government to punish minor drug offenders without giving the offender a criminal record if the offender is in possession of only a small amount of drugs. This law is designed to impact the "user" of illicit drugs, while simultaneously saving the government the costs of a full-blown criminal investigation.

Under this section, the government has the option of imposing only a civil fine on individuals possessing only a small quantity of an illegal drug. Possession of this small quantity, identified as a "personal use amount" carries a civil fine of up to $10,000.

In determining the amount of the fine in a particular case, the drug offender's income and assets will be considered. This is accomplished through an administrative proceeding rather than a criminal trial, thus reducing the exposure of the offender to the entire criminal justice system, and reducing the costs to the offender and the government.

The value of this section is that it allows the government to punish a minor drug offender without saddling the offender with a criminal record. This section also gives the drug offender the opportunity to fully redeem himself or herself, and have all public record of the proceeding destroyed. If this was the drug offender's first offense, and the offender has paid all fines, can pass a drug test, and has not been convicted of a crime after three years, the offender can request that all proceedings be dismissed.

If the proceeding is dismissed, the drug offender can lawfully say he or she had never been prosecuted, either criminally or civilly, for a drug offense.

Congress has imposed two limitations on this section's use. It may not be used if (1) the drug offender has been previously convicted of a Federal or state drug offense; or (2) the offender has already been fined twice under this section.

NARCOTICS

The term narcotic, derived from the Greek word for stupor, originally referred to a variety of substances that induced sleep. In a legal context, narcotic refers to opium, opium derivatives and their semisynthetic or totally synthetic substitutes. Cocaine and coca leaves, which are classified as "narcotics" in the Controlled Substances Act (CSA), are technically not narcotics and are discussed in the section on stimulants.

Narcotics can be administered in a variety of ways. Some are taken orally, transdermally (skin patches) or injected. They are also available in suppositories. As drugs of abuse, they are often smoked, sniffed or self-administered by the more direct routes of subcutaneous ("skin popping") and intravenous ("mainlining") injection.

Drug effects depend heavily on the dose, route of administration, previous exposure to the drug and the expectation of the user. Aside from their clinical use in the treatment of pain, cough suppression and acute diarrhea, narcotics produce a general sense of well-being by reducing tension, anxiety, and aggression. These effects are helpful in a therapeutic setting but contribute to their abuse.

Narcotic use is associated with a variety of unwanted effects including drowsiness, inability to concentrate, apathy, lessened physical activity, constriction of the pupils, dilation of the subcutaneous blood vessels causing flushing of the face and neck, constipation, nausea and vomiting and, most significantly, respiratory depression. As the dose is increased, the subjective, analgesic, and toxic effects become more pronounced. Except in cases of acute intoxication, there is no loss of motor coordination or slurred speech as occurs with many depressants.

Among the hazards of illicit drug use is the ever increasing risk of infection, disease and overdose. Medical complications common among narcotic abusers arise primarily from adulterants found in street drugs and in the non-sterile practices of injecting. Skin, lung and brain abscesses, endocarditis, hepatitis and AIDS are commonly found among narcotic abusers. Since there is no simple way to determine the purity of a drug that is sold on the street, the effects of illicit narcotic use are unpredictable and can be fatal.

With repeated use of narcotics, tolerance and dependence develop. The development of tolerance is characterized by a shortened duration and a decreased intensity of analgesia, euphoria and sedation which creates the need to administer progressively larger doses to attain the desired effect. Tolerance does not develop uniformly for all actions of these drugs, giving rise to a number of toxic effects. Although the lethal dose is increased significantly in tolerant users, there is always a dose at which death can occur from respiratory depression.

Physical dependence refers to an alteration of nor" mal body functions that necessitates the continued presence of a drug in order to prevent the withdrawal or abstinence syndrome. The intensity and character of the physical symptoms experienced during withdrawal are directly related to the particular drug of abuse, the total daily dose, the interval between doses, the duration of use and the health and personality of the addict. In general, narcotics with shorter durations of action tend to produce shorter, more intense withdrawal symptoms, while drugs that produce longer narcotic effects have prolonged symptoms that tend to be less severe.

The withdrawal symptoms experienced from heroin/morphine-like addiction are usually experienced shortly before the time of the next scheduled dose. Early symptoms include watery eyes, runny nose, yawning and sweating. Restlessness, irritability, loss of appetite, tremors and severe sneezing appear as the syndrome progresses. Severe depression and vomiting are not uncommon. The heart rate and blood pressure are elevated. Chills alternating with flushing and excessive sweating are also characteristic symptoms. Pains in the bones and muscles of the back and extremities occur as do muscle spasms and kicking movements, which may be the source of the expression "kicking the habit." At any point during this process, a suitable narcotic can be administered that will dramatically reverse the withdrawal symptoms. Without intervention, the syndrome will run its course and most of the overt physical symptoms will disappear within 7 to 10 days.

The psychological dependence that is associated with narcotic addiction is complex and protracted. Long after the physical need for the drug has passed, the addict may continue to think and talk about the use of drugs. There is a high probability that relapse will occur after narcotic withdrawal when neither the physical environment nor the behavioral motivators that contributed to the abuse have been altered.

There are two major patterns of narcotic abuse or dependence seen in the U.S. One involves individuals whose drug use was initiated within the context of medical treatment who escalate their dose through "doctor shopping" or branch out to illicit drugs. A very small percentage of addicts are in this group

The other more common pattern of abuse is initiated outside the therapeutic setting with experimental or recreational use of narcotics. The majority of individuals in this category may abuse narcotics sporadically for months or even years. These occasional users are called "chippers." Although they are neither tolerant of nor dependent on narcotics, the social, medical and legal consequences of their behavior is very serious. Some experimental users will escalate their narcotic use and will eventually become dependent, both physically and psychologically. The earlier drug use begins, the more likely it is to progress to abuse and dependence. Heroin use among males in inner cities is generally initiated in adolescence and dependence develops in about 1or 2 years.

Narcotics of Natural Origin

The poppy *Papaver somniferum* is the source for non-synthetic narcotics. It was grown in the Mediterranean region as early as 5000 B.C., and has since been cultivated in a number of countries throughout the world. The milky fluid that seeps from incisions in the unripe seedpod of this poppy has, since ancient times, been scraped by hand and air dried to produce what is known as opium. A more modern method of harvesting is by the industrial poppy straw process of extracting alkaloids from the mature dried plant. The extract may be in liquid, solid or powder form, although most poppy straw concentrate available commercially is a fine brownish powder. More than 500 tons of opium or their equivalents in poppy straw concentrate are legally imported into the U.S. annually for legitimate medical use.

Opium - There were no legal restrictions on the importation or use of opium until the early 1900s. In the United States, the unrestricted availability of opium, the influx of opium smoking immigrants from the Orient, and the invention of the hypodermic needle contributed to the more severe variety of compulsive drug abuse seen at the turn of this century. In those days, medicines often contained opium without any warning label. Today there are state, federal and international laws governing the production and distribution of narcotic substances.

Although opium is used in the form of paragoric to treat diarrhea, most opium imported into the United States is broken down into its alkaloid constituents. These alkaloids are divided into two distinct chemical classes, phenanthrenes and isoquinolines. The principal phenanthrenes are morphine, codeine and thebaine, while the isoquinolines have no significant central nervous system effects and are not regulated under the CSA.

Morphine - Morphine, the principal constituent of opium, can range in concentration from 4 to 21 percent (note: commercial opium is standardized to contain 10% morphine). It is one of the most effective drugs known for the relief of pain, and remains the standard against which new analgesics are measured. Morphine is marketed in a variety of forms including oral solutions (Roxanol), sustained release tablets (MSIR and MS-Contin), suppositories and injectable preparations. It may be administered orally, subcutaneously, intramuscularly, or intravenously, the latter method being the one most frequently used by addicts. Tolerance and physical dependence develop rapidly in the user. Only a small part of the morphine obtained from opium is used directly; most of it is converted to codeine and other derivatives.

Codeine - This alkaloid is found in opium in concentrations ranging from 0.7 to 2.5 percent. Most codeine used in the U.S. is produced from morphine. Compared to morphine, codeine produces less analgesia, sedation and respiratory depression and is frequently taken orally. Codeine is medically prescribed for the relief of moderate pain. It is made into tablets either alone or in combination with aspirin or acetaminophen (Tylenol). Codeine is an effective cough suppressant and is found in a number of liquid preparations. Codeine products are also used to a lesser extent, as an injectable solution for the treatment of pain. It is by far the most widely used naturally occurring narcotic in medical treatment in the world. Codeine products are encountered on the illicit market frequently in combination with glutethimide (Doriden) or carisoprodol (Soma).

Thebaine - A minor constituent of opium, thebaine is chemically similar to both morphine and codeine, but produces stimulatory rather than depressant effects. Thebaine is not used therapeutically, but is converted into a variety of compounds including codeine, hydrocodone, oxycodone, oxymorphone, nalbuphine, naloxone, naltrexone and buprenorphine. It is controlled in Schedule II of the CSA as well as under international law.

Semi-Synthetic Narcotics

The following narcotics are among the more significant substances that have been derived by modification of the phenanthrene alkaloids contained in opium:

Heroin - First synthesized from morphine in 1874, heroin was not extensively used in medicine until the beginning of this century. Commercial production of the new pain remedy was first started in 1898. While it received widespread acceptance from the medical profession, physicians remained unaware of its potential for addiction for years. The first comprehensive control of heroin in the United States was established with the Harrison Narcotic Act of 1914.

Pure heroin is a white powder with a bitter taste. Most illicit heroin is a powder which may vary in color from white to dark brown because of impurities left from the manufacturing process or the presence of additives. Pure heroin is rarely sold on the street. A "bag"-slang for a single dosage unit of heroin-may contain 100 mg of powder, only a portion of which is heroin; the remainder could be sugars, starch, powdered milk, or quinine. Traditionally the purity of heroin in a bag has ranged from 1 to 10 percent; more recently heroin purity has ranged from 1 to 98 percent, with a national average of 35 percent.

Another form of heroin known as "black tar" has also become increasingly available in the western United States. The color and consistency of black tar heroin result from the crude processing methods used to illicitly manufacture heroin in Mexico. Black tar heroin may be sticky like roofing tar or hard like coal, and its color may vary from dark brown to black. Black tar heroin is often sold on the street in its tar-like state at purities ranging from 20 to 80 percent. Black tar heroin is most frequently dissolved, diluted and injected.

The typical heroin user today consumes more heroin than a typical user did just a decade ago, which is not surprising given the higher purity currently available at the street level. Until recently, heroin in the United States almost exclusively was injected either intravenously, subcutaneously (skin-popping), or intramuscularly. Injection is the most practical and efficient way to administer low-purity heroin. The availability of higher purity heroin has meant that users now can snort or smoke the narcotic. Evidence suggests that heroin snorting is widespread or increasing in those areas of the country where high-purity heroin is available, generally in the northeastern United States. This method of administration may be more appealing to new users because it eliminates both the fear of acquiring syringe-borne diseases such as HIV / AIDS and hepatitis, and the historical stigma attached to intravenous heroin use.

Hydromorphone - Hydromorphone (Dilaudid) is marketed both in tablet and injectable forms. Its analgesic potency is from two to eight times that of morphine. Much sought after by narcotic addicts, hydromorphone is usually obtained by the abuser through fraudulent prescriptions or theft. The tablets are dissolved and injected as a substitute for heroin

Oxycodone - Oxycodone is synthesized from thebaine. It is similar to codeine, but is more potent and has a higher dependence potential. It is effective orally and is marketed in combination with aspirin (Percodan) or acetaminophen (Percocet) for the relief of pain. Addicts take these tablets orally or dissolve them in water, filter out the insoluble material, and "mainline" the active drug.

Hydrocodone - Hydrocodone is an orally active analgesic and antitussive Schedule II narcotic which is marketed in multi-ingredient Schedule III products. The therapeutic dose of 5-10 mg is pharmacologically equivalent to 60 mg of oral morphine. Sales and production of this drug have increased significantly in recent years as have diversion and illicit use. Trade names include Anexsia, Hycodan, Hycomine, Lorcet, Lortab, Tussionex, Tylox and Vicodin. These are available as tablets, capsules and/or syrups.

Synthetic Narcotics

In contrast to the pharmaceutical products derived directly or indirectly from narcotics of natural origin, synthetic narcotics are produced entirely within the laboratory. The continuing search for products that retain the analgesic properties of morphine without the consequent dangers of tolerance and dependence has yet to yield a product that is not susceptible to abuse. A number of clandestinely-produced drugs as well as drugs that have accepted medical uses fall into this category.

Meperidine - Introduced as a potent analgesic in the 1930s, meperidine produces effects that are similar but not identical to morphine (shorter duration of action and reduced antitussive and antidiarrheal actions). Currently it is used for the relief of moderate to severe pain, particularly in obstetrics and post-operative situations. Meperdine is available in tablets, syrups and injectable forms (Demerol). Several analogues of meperidine have been clandestinely produced. One noteworthy analogue is a preparation with a neurotoxic by-product that has produced irreversible Parkinsonism.

Methadone and Related Drugs - German scientist's synthesized methadone during World War II because of a shortage of morphine. Although chemically unlike morphine or heroin, methadone produces many of the same effects. Introduced into the United States in 1947 as an analgesic (Dolophine), it is primarily used today for the treatment of narcotic addiction (Methadone). The effects of methadone are longer-lasting than those of morphine based drugs. Methadone's effects can last up to 24 hours, thereby permitting administration only once a day in heroin detoxification and maintenance programs. Methadone is almost as effective when administered orally as it is by injection. Tolerance and dependence may develop, and withdrawal symptoms, though they develop more slowly and are less severe than those of morphine and more slowly and are less severe than those of morphine and heroin, are more prolonged. Ironically, methadone used to control narcotic addiction is frequently encountered on the illicit market and has been associated with a number of overdose deaths.

Closely related to methadone, the synthetic compound levo-alphacetylmethadol or LAAM (ORLAAM) has an even longer duration of action (from 48 to 72 hours), permitting a reduction in frequency of use. In 1994 it was approved as a treatment of narcotic addiction. Buprenorphine (Buprenex), a semi-synthetic Schedule V narcotic analgesic derived from thebaine, is currently being investigated as a treatment of narcotic addiction.

Another close relative of methadone is dextropropoxyphene, first marketed in 1957 under the trade name of Darvon. Oral analgesic potency is one-half to one-third that of codeine, with 65 mg approximately equivalent to about 600 mg of aspirin. Dextroproxyphene is prescribed for relief of mild to moderate pain. Bulk dextropropoxyphene is in Schedule II, while preparations containing it are in Schedule IV. More than 100 tons of dextropropoxyphene are produced in the U.S. annually, and more than 25 million prescriptions are written for the products. This narcotic is associated with a number of toxic side effects and is among the top 10 drugs reported by medical examiners in drug abuse deaths.

Fentanyl - First synthesized in Belgium in the late 1950s, fentanyl was introduced into clinical practice in the 1960s as an intravenous anesthetic under the trade name of Sublimaze. Thereafter, two other fentanyl analogues were introduced: alfentanil (Alfenta), an ultra-short (5-10 minutes) acting analgesic, and sufentanil (Sufenta), an exceptionally potent analgesic for use in heart surgery. Today fentanyls are extensively used for anesthesia and analgesia. Illicit use of pharmaceutical fentanyls first appeared in the mid-1970s in the medical community and continues to be a problem in the U.S. To date, over 12 different analogues of fentanyl have been produced clandestinely and identified in the U.S. drug traffic. The biological effects of the fentanyls are indistinguishable from those of heroin with the exception that the fentanyls may be hundreds of times more potent. Fentanyls are most commonly used by intravenous administration, but like heroin, they may be smoked or snorted.

Pentazocine - The effort to find an effective analgesic that is less dependence-producing led to the development of pentazocine (Tal win). Introduced as an analgesic in 1967, it was frequently encountered in the illicit trade, usually in combination with tripelennamine and placed into Schedule IV in 1979. An attempt at reducing the abuse of this drug was made with the introduction of Talwin Nx. This product contains a quantity of antagonist sufficient to counteract the morphine-like effects of pentazocine if the tablets are dissolved and injected.

DEPRESSANTS

Historically, people of almost every culture have used chemical agents to induce sleep, relieve stress, and allay anxiety. While alcohol is one of the oldest and most universal agents used for these purposes, hundreds of substances have been developed that produce central nervous system (CNS) depression. These drugs have been referred to as "downers," sedatives, hypnotics, minor tranquilizers, anxiolytics, and antianxiety medications. Unlike most other classes of drugs of abuse, depressants, except for methaqualone, are rarely produced in clandestine laboratories. Generally, legitimate pharmaceutical products are diverted to the illicit market.

Although a number of depressants (i.e., chloral hydrate, glutethimide, meprobamate and methaqualone) have been important players in the milieu of depressant use and abuse, two major groups of depressants have dominated the licit and illicit market for nearly a century, first barbiturates and now benzodiazepines.

Barbiturates were very popular in the first half of this century. In moderate amounts, these drugs produce a state of intoxication that is remarkably similar to alcohol intoxication. Symptoms include slurred speech, loss of motor coordination and impaired judgment. Depending on the dose, frequency, and duration of use, one can rapidly develop tolerance, physical dependence and psychological dependence on barbiturates. With the development of tolerance, the margin of safety between the effective dose and the lethal dose becomes very narrow. That is, in order to obtain the same level of intoxication, the tolerant abuser may raise his or her dose to a level that can produce coma and death. Although many individuals have taken barbiturates therapeutically without harm, concern about the addiction potential of barbiturates and the ever-increasing numbers of fatalities associated with them led to the development of alternative medications. Today, only about 20% of all depressant prescriptions in the U.S. are for barbiturates.

Benzodiazepines were first marketed in the 1960s. Touted as much safer depressants with far less addiction potential than barbiturates, these drugs today account for about 30% of all prescriptions for controlled substances. It has only been recently that an awareness has developed that benzodiazepines share many of the undesirable side effects of the barbiturates. A number of toxic CNS effects are seen with chronic high dose benzodiazepine therapy. These include headache, irritability, confusion, memory impairment, depression, insomnia and tremor. The risk of developing over-sedation, dizziness and confusion increases substantially with higher doses of benzodiazepines. Prolonged use can lead to physical dependence even at recommended dosages. Unlike barbiturates, large doses of benzodiazepines are rarely fatal unless combined with other drugs or alcohol. Although primary abuse of benzodiazepines is well documented, abuse of these drugs usually occurs as part of a pattern of multiple drug abuse. For example, heroin or cocaine abusers will use benzodiazepines and other depressants to augment their "high" or alter the side effects associated with over-stimulation or narcotic withdrawal.

There are marked similarities among the withdrawal symptoms seen with all drugs classified as depressants. In its mildest form, the withdrawal syndrome may produce insomnia and anxiety, usually the same symptoms that initiated the drug use. With a greater level of dependence, tremors and weakness are also present, and in its most severe form, the withdrawal syndrome can cause seizures and delirium. Unlike the withdrawal syndrome seen with most other drugs of abuse, withdrawal from depressants can be life-threatening

Chloral Hydrate

The oldest of the hypnotic (sleep inducing) depressants, chloral hydrate was first synthesized in 1832. Marketed as syrups or soft gelatin capsules, chloral hydrate takes effect in a relatively short time (30 minutes) and will induce sleep in about an hour. A solution of chloral hydrate and alcohol
constituted the infamous "knockout drops" or "Mickey Finn." At therapeutic doses, chloral· hydrate has little effect on respiration and blood pressure but, a toxic dose produces severe respiratory depression and very low blood pressure. Although chloral hydrate is still encountered today, its use declined with the introduction of the barbiturates

Barbiturates

Barbiturates (derivatives of barbituric acid) were first introduced for medical use in the early 1900s. More than 2,500 barbiturates have been synthesized, and in the height of their popularity about 50 were marketed for human use. Today, only about a dozen are used. Barbiturates produce a wide spectrum of CNS depression, from mild sedation to coma, and have been used as sedatives, hypnotics, anesthetics and anticonvulsants.

The primary differences among many of these products are how fast they produce an effect and how long those effects last. Barbiturates are classified as ultrashort, short, intermediate and long-acting.

The ultrashort-acting barbiturates produce anesthesia within about one minute after intravenous administration. Those in current medical use are methohexital (Brevital), thiamylal (Surital) and thiopental (Pentothal).

Barbiturate abusers prefer the short-acting and intermediate-acting barbiturates pentobarbital (Nembutal), secobarbital (Seconal) and amobarbital (Amytal). Other short- and intermediate-acting barbiturates are butalbital (Fiorinal, Fioricet), butabarbital (Butisol), talbutal (Lotusate) and aprobarbital (Alurate). After oral administration, the onset of action is from 15 to 40 minutes and the effects last up to 6 hours. These drugs are primarily used for sedation or to induce sleep. Veterinarians use pentobarbital for anesthesia and euthanasia.

Long-acting barbiturates include phenobarbital (Luminal) and mephobarbital (Mebaral). Effects of these drugs are realized in about one hour and last for about 12 hours and are used primarily for daytime sedation and the treatment of seizure disorders or mild anxiety.

Glutethimide and Methqualone

Glutethimide (Doriden) was introduced in 1954 and methaqualone (Quaa1ude, Sopor) in 1965 as safe barbiturate substitutes. Experience showed, however, that their addiction liability and the severity of withdrawal symptoms were similar to those of barbiturates. By 1972, "luding out," taking methaqualone with wine, was a popular college pastime. Excessive use leads to tolerance, dependence and withdrawal symptoms similar to those of barbiturates. Overdose by glutethimide and methaqualone is more difficult to treat than barbiturate overdose, and deaths have frequently occurred. In the United States, the marketing of methaqualone pharmaceutical products stopped in 1984 and methaqualone was transferred to Schedule I of the CSA. In 1991, glutethimide was transferred into Schedule II in response to an upsurge in the prevalence of diversion, abuse and overdose deaths.

Meprobamate

Meprobamate was introduced as an antianxiety agent in 1955 and is prescribed primarily to treat anxiety, tension and associated muscle spasms. More than 50 tons are distributed annually in the U.S. under its generic name and brand names such as Miltown and Equanil. Its onset and duration of action are similar to the intermediate acting barbiturates; however, therapeutic doses of meprobamate produce less sedation and toxicity than barbiturates. Excessive use can result in psychological and physical dependence.

Benzodiazepines

The benzodiazepine family of depressants is used therapeutically to produce sedation, induce sleep, relieve anxiety and muscle spasms and to prevent seizures. In general, benzodiazepines act as hypnotics in high doses, as anxiolytics in moderate doses and as sedatives in low doses. Of the drugs marketed in the United States that affect CNS function, benzodiazepines are among the widely prescribed medications and, unfortunately, are frequently abused. Fifteen members of this group are presently marketed in the United States and an additional twenty are marketed in other countries.

Like the barbiturates, benzodiazepines differ from one another in how fast they take effect and how long the effects last. Shorter acting benzodiazepines, used to manage insomnia, include estazolam (ProSom), flurazepam (Dalmane), quazepam (Doral), temazepam (Restoril) and triazolam (Halcion).

Benzodiazepines with longer durations of action include alprazolam (Xanax), chlordiazepoxide (Librium), clorazepate (Tranxene), diazepam (Valium), halazepam (Paxipam), lorazepam (Ativan), oxazepam (Serax) and prazepam (Centrax). These longer acting drugs are primarily used for the treatment of general anxiety. Midazolam (Versed) is available in the U.S. only in an injectable form for an adjunct to anesthesia. Clonazepam (Klonopin) is recommended for use in the treatment of seizure disorders.

Flunitrazepam (Rohypnol), which produces diazepam-like effects, is becoming increasingly popular among young people as a drug of abuse. The drug is not marketed legally in the United States, but is smuggled in by traffickers.

Benzodiazepines are classified in the CSA as Schedule IV depressants. Repeated use of large doses or, in some cases, daily use of therapeutic doses of benzodiazepines is associated with physical dependence. The withdrawal syndrome is similar to that of alcohol withdrawal and is generally more unpleasant and longer lasting than narcotic withdrawal and frequently requires hospitalization. Abrupt cessation of benzodiazepines is not recommended and tapering-down the dose eliminates many of the unpleasant symptoms.

Given the number of people who are prescribed benzodiazepines, relatively few patients increase their dosage or engage in drugseeking behavior. However, those individuals who do abuse benzodiazepines often maintain their drug supply by getting prescriptions from several doctors, forging prescriptions or buying diverted pharmaceutical products on the illicit market. Abuse is frequently associated with adolescents and young adults who take benzodiazepines to obtain a "high." This intoxicated state results in reduced inhibition and impaired judgment. Concurrent use of a1cohol or other depressants with benzodiazepines can be life-threatening. Abuse of benzodiazepines is particularly high among heroin and cocaine abusers. Approximately 50 percent of people entering treatment for narcotic or cocaine addiction also report abusing benzodiazepines.

STIMULANTS

Stimulants are sometimes referred to as "uppers" and reverse the effects of fatigue on both mental and physical tasks. Two commonly used stimulants are nicotine, found in tobacco products, and caffeine, an active ingredient in coffee, tea, some soft drinks and many non-prescription medicines. Used in moderation, these substances tend to relieve malaise and increase alertness. Although the use of these products has been an accepted part of our culture, the recognition of their adverse effects has resulted in a proliferation of caffeine-free products and efforts to discourage cigarette smoking.

A number of stimulants, however, are under the regulatory control of the CSA. Some of these controlled substances are available by prescription for legitimate medical use in the treatment of obesity, narcolepsy and attention deficit hyperactivity disorders. As drugs of abuse, stimulants are frequently taken to produce a sense of exhilaration, enhance self-esteem, improve mental and physical performance, increase activity, reduce appetite, produce prolonged wakefulness, and to "get high." They are recognized as among the most potent agents of reward and reinforcement that underlie the problem of dependence.

Stimulants are both diverted from legitimate channels and clandestinely manufactured exclusively for the illicit market. They are taken orally, sniffed, smoked and injected. Smoking, snorting or injecting stimulants produces a sudden sensation known. as a "rush" or a "flash." Abuse is often associated with a pattern of binge use that is, consuming large doses of stimulants sporadically. Heavy users may inject themselves every few hours, continuing until they have depleted their drug supply or reached a point of delirium, psychosis and physical exhaustion. During this period of heavy use, all other interests become secondary to recreating the initial euphoric rush. Tolerance can develop rapidly, and both physical and psychological dependence occur. Abrupt cessation, even after a weekend binge, is commonly followed by depression, anxiety, drug craving and extreme fatigue ("crash").

Therapeutic levels of stimulants can produce exhilaration, extended wakefulness and loss of appetite. These effects are greatly intensified when large doses of stimulants are taken. Physical side effects-including dizziness, tremor, headache, flushed skin, chest pain with palpitations, excessive sweating, vomiting and abdominal cramps-may occur as a result of taking too large a dose at one time or taking large doses over an extended period of time. Psychological effects include agitation, hostility, panic, aggression and suicidal or homicidal tendencies. Paranoia, sometimes accompanied by both auditory and visual hallucinations, may also occur. In overdose, unless there is medical intervention, high fever, convulsions and car- diovascular collapse may precede death. Because accidental death is partially due to the effects of stimulants on the body's cardiovascular and temperature-regulating systems, physical exertion increases the hazards of stimulant use.

Cocaine

Cocaine, the most potent stimulant of natural origin, is extracted from the leaves of the coca plant (Erythroxylon coca) which is indigenous to the Andean highlands of South America. Natives in this region chew or brew coca leaves into a tea for refreshment and to relieve fatigue similar to the customs of chewing tobacco and drinking tea or coffee.

Pure cocaine was first isolated in the 1880s and used as a local anesthetic in eye surgery. It was particularly useful in surgery of the nose and throat because of its ability to provide   anesth-

anesthesia as well as to constrict blood vessels and limit bleeding. Many of its therapeutic applications are now obsolete due to the development of safer drugs.

Illicit cocaine is usually distributed as a white crystalline powder or as an off-white chunky material. The powder, usually cocaine hydrochloride, is often diluted with a variety of substances, the most common of which are sugars such as lactose, inositol and mannitol, and local anesthetics such as lidocaine. The adulteration increases the volume and thus multiplies profits. Cocaine hydrochloride is generally snorted or dissolved in water and injected. It is rarely smoked.

"Crack," the chunk or "rock" form of cocaine, is a ready-to-use freebase. On the illicit market it is sold in small, inexpensive dosage units that are smoked. With crack came a dramatic increase in drug abuse problems and violence. Smoking delivers large quantities of cocaine to the lungs producing effects comparable to intravenous injection; these effects are felt almost immediately after smoking, are very intense, and are quickly over. Once introduced in the mid-1980s, crack abuse spread rapidly and made the cocaine experience available to anyone with $10 and access to a dealer. In addition to other toxicities associated with cocaine abuse, cocaine smokers suffer from acute respiratory problems including cough, shortness of breath, and severe chest painswitll lung trauma and bleeding.

The intensity of the psychological effects of cocaine, as with most psychoactive drugs, depends on the dose and rate of entry to the brain. Cocaine reaches the brain through the snorting method in three to five minutes. Intravenous injection of cocaine produces a rush in 15 to 30 seconds and smoking produces an almost immediate intense experience. The euphoric effects of cocaine are almost indistinguishable from those of amphetamine, although they do not last as long. These intense effects can be followed by a dysphoric crash. To avoid the fatigue and the depression of "coming down," frequent repeated doses are taken. Excessive doses of cocaine may lead to seizures and death from respiratory failure, stroke, cerebral hemorrhage or heart failure. There is no specific antidote for cocaine overdose.

According to the 1993 Household Drug Survey, the number of Americans who used cocaine within the preceding month of the survey numbered about 1.3 million; occasional users (those who used cocaine less often than monthly) numbered at approximately 3 million, down from 8.1 million in 1985. The number of weekly users has remained steady at around a half million since 1983.

Amphetamines

Amphetamine, dextroamphetamine and methamphetamine are collectively referred to as amphetamines. Their chemical properties and actions are so similar that even experienced users have difficulty knowing which drug they have taken.

Amphetamine was first marketed in the 1930s as Benzedrine in an over-the-counter inhaler to treat nasal congestion. By 1937 amphetamine was available by prescription in tablet form and was used in the treatment of the sleeping disorder narcolepsy and the behavioral syndrome called minimal brain dysfunction (MBD), which today is called attention deficit hyperactivity disorder (ADHD). During World War II, amphetamine was widely used to keep the fighting men going; both dextroamphetamine (Dexedrine) and methamphetamine (Methedrine) became readily available. As use of amphetamines spread, so did their abuse. Amphetamines became a cureall for helping truckers to complete their long routes without falling asleep, for weight control, for helping athletes to perform better and train longer, and for treating mild depression. Intravenous amphetamine abuse spread among a subculture known as "speed freaks." With experience, it became evident that the dangers of abuse of these drugs outweighed most of their therapeutic uses.

Increased control measures were initiated in 1965 with amendments to the federal food and drug laws to curb the black market in amphetamines. Many pharmaceutical amphetamine products were removed from the market and doctors prescribed those that remained less freely. In order to

meet the everincreasing black market demand for amphetamines, clandestine laboratory's. production mushroomed, especially methamphetamine laboratories on the West Coast. Today, most amphetamines distributed to the black market are produced in clandestine laboratories.

Amphetamines are generally taken orally or injected. However, the addition of "ice," the slang name for crystallized methamphetamine hydrochloride, has promoted smoking as another mode of administration. Just as "crack" is smokable cocaine, "ice" is smokable methamphetamine. Both drugs are highly addictive and toxic.

The effects of amphetamines, especially methamphetamine, are similar to cocaine, but their onset is slower and their duration is longer. In general, chronic abuse produces a psychosis that resembles schizophrenia and is characterized by paranoia, picking at the skin, preoccupation with one's own thoughts, and auditory and visual hallucinations. Violent and erratic behavior is frequently seen among chronic abusers of amphetamines.

Methcathinone

Methcathinone is one of the more recent drugs of abuse in the U.S. and was placed into Schedule I of the CSA in 1993. Known on the streets as "Cat," it is a structural analogue of methamphetamine and cathinone. Clandestinely manufactured, methcathinone is almost exclusively sold in the stable and highly water soluble hydrochloride salt form. It is most commonly snorted, although it can be taken orally by mixing it with a beverage or diluted in water and injected intravenously. Methcathinone has an abuse potential equivalent to methamphetamine, and produces amphetamine-like activity including superabundant energy, hyperactivity, extended wakefulness and loss of appetite. Pleasant effects include a burst of energy, speeding of the mind, increased feelings of invincibility and euphoria. Unpleasant effects include anxiety, tremor, insomnia, weight loss, dehydration, sweating, stomach pains, pounding heart, nose bleeds and body aches. Toxic levels may produce convulsions, paranoia, and hallucinations. Like other CNS stimulants, binges are usually followed by a "crash" with periods of variable depression.

Khat

For centuries, khat, the fresh young leaves of the Catha edulis shrub, has been consumed where the plant is cultivated, primarily in East Africa and the Arabian Peninsula. There, chewing khat predates the use of coffee and is used in a similar social context. Chewed in moderation, khat alleviates fatigue and reduces appetite. Compulsive use may result in manic behavior with grandiose delusions or in a paranoid type of illness, some- times accompanied by hallucinations.

Khat has been brought into the U.S. and other countries for use by emigrants from the source countries. It contains a number of chemicals among which are two controlled substances, cathinone (Schedule I) and cathine (Schedule IV). As the leaves mature or dry, cathinone is converted to cathine which significantly reduces its stimulatory properties.

Methylphenidate (Ritalin)

The primary, legitimate medical use of methylphenidate (Ritalin) is to treat attention deficit disorders in children. As with other Schedule II stimulants, the abuse of methylphenidate may produce the same effects as the abuse of cocaine or the amphetamines. It has been reported that the psychosis of chronic methylphenidate intoxication is identical to the paranoid psychosis of amphetamine intoxication. Unlike other stimulants, however, methylphenidate has not been clandestinely produced, although abuse of this substance has been well documented among narcotic addicts who dissolve the tablets in water and inject the mixture. Complications arising from this practice are common due to the insoluble fillers used in the tablets. When injected, these materials block small blood vessels, causing serious damage to the lung and retina of the eye.

Anorectic Drugs

A number of drugs have been developed and marketed to replace amphetamines as appetite suppressants. These anorectic drugs include benzphetamine (Didrex), diethylproprion (Tenuate, Tepanil), fenfluramine (Pondimin), mazindol (Sanorex, Mazanor), phendimetrazine (Bontril, Prelu-l, Plegine) and phentermine (Ionamin, AdipexP). They produce many of the effects of the amphetamines, but are generally less potent. All are controlled under the CSA because of the similarity of their effects to those of the amphetamines.

HALLUCINOGENS

Hallucinogens are among the oldest known group of drugs that have been used for their ability to alter human perception and mood. For centuries, many of the naturally occurring hallucinogens found in plants and fungi have been used for medical, social, and religious practices. In more recent years, a number of synthetic hallucinogens have been produced, some of which are much more potent than their naturally occurring counterparts.

The biochemical, pharmacological and physiological basis for hallucinogenic activity is not well understood. Even the name for this class of drugs is not ideal, since hallucinogens do not always produce hallucinations. However, taken in nontoxic dosages, these substances produce changes in perception, thought and mood. Physiological effects include elevated heart rate, increased blood pressure and dilated pupils. Sensory effects include perceptual distortions that vary with dose, setting and mood. Psychic effects include disorders of thought associated with time and space. Time may appear to stand still and forms and colors seem to change and take on new significance. This experience may be pleasurable or extremely frightening. It needs to be stressed that the effects of hallucinogens are unpredictable each time they are used.

Weeks or even months after some hallucinogens have been taken; the user may experience flashbacks-fragmentary recurrences of certain aspects of the drug experience in the absence of actually taking the drug. The occurrence of a flashback is unpredictable, but is more likely to occur during times of stress and seem to occur more frequently in younger individuals. With time, these episodes diminish and become less intense.

The abuse of hallucinogens in the United States reached a peak in the late 1960s. A subsequent decline in their use may be attributed to real or perceived hazards associated with taking these drugs. However, a resurgence of use of hallucinogens in the 1990s, especially at the junior high school level, is cause for concern.

There is a considerable body of literature that links the use of some of the hallucinogenic substances to neuronal damage in animals; however, there is no conclusive scientific data that links brain or chromosomal damage to the use of hallucinogens in humans. The most common danger of hallucinogen use is impaired judgment that often leads to rash decisions and accidents.

NATURALLY OCCURRING HALLUCINOGENS

Peyote and Mescaline

Peyote is a small, spineless cactus, Lophophora williamsii, whose principal active ingredient is the hallucinogen mescaline. From earliest recorded time, peyote has been used by natives in northern Mexico and southwestern United States as a part of traditional religious rites. The top of the cactus above ground-also referred to as the crown-consists of disc-shaped buttons that are cut from the roots and dried. These buttons are generally chewed or soaked in water to produce an intoxicating liquid. The hallucinogenic dose for mescaline is about 0.3 to 0.5 grams (equivalent to about 5 grams of dried peyote) and lasts about 12 hours. While peyote produced rich visual hallucinations which were important to the native peyote cults, the full spectrum of effects served as a chemically induced model of mental illness. Mescaline can be extracted from peyote or produced synthetically.

Psilocybin and Psilocyn

Psilocybin and psilocyn are both chemicals obtained from certain mushrooms found in Mexico and Central America. Like peyote, the mushrooms have been used in native rites for centuries. Dried mushrooms contain about 0.2 to 0.4 percent psilocybin and only trace amounts of psilocyn. The hallucinogenic dose of both substances is about 4 to 8 milligrams or about 2 grams of mushrooms with effects lasting for about six hours. Both psilocybin and psilocyn can be produced synthetically.

Dimethyltryptamine (DMT)

Dimethyltryptamine, (DMT) has a long history of use worldwide as it is found in a variety of plants and seeds and can also be produced synthetically. It is ineffective when taken orally unless combined with another drug that inhibits its metabolism. Generally it is sniffed, smoked or injected. The effective hallucinogenic dose in humans is about 50 to 100 milligrams and lasts for about 45 to 60 minutes. Because the effects last only about an hour, the experience was called a "businessman's trip."

A number of other hallucinogens have very similar structures and properties to those of DMT. Diethyltryptamine (DET), for example, is an analogue of DMT and produces the same pharmacological effects but is somewhat less potent than DMT. Alphaethyltryptamine (AET) is another tryptamine hallucinogen recently added to the list of Schedule I substances in the CSA.

LSD

Lysergic acid diethylamide (LSD) is the most potent and highly studied hallucinogen known to man. It was originally synthesized in 1938 by Dr. Albert Hoffman, but its hallucinogenic effects were unknown until 1943 when Hoffman accidently consumed some LSD. It was later found that an oral dose of as little as 0.025 mg (or 25 micrograms, equal to a few grains of salt) was capable of producing rich and vivid hallucinations.

Because of its structural similarity to a chemical present in the brain and its similarity in effects to certain aspects of psychosis, LSD was used as a research tool to study mental illness. Although there was a decline in its illicit use from its initial popularity in the 1960s, LSD is making a comeback in the 1990s. The average effective oral dose is from 20 to 80 micrograms with the effects of higher doses lasting for 10 to 12 hours. LSD is usually sold in the form of impregnated paper (blotter acid), tablets (microdots), or thin squares of gelatin (window panes).

Physical reactions may include dilated pupils, lowered body temperature, nausea, "goose bumps," profuse perspiration, increased blood sugar and rapid heart rate. During the first hour after ingestion, the user may experience visual changes with extreme changes in mood. In the hallucinatory state, the user may suffer impaired depth and time perception accompanied by distorted perception of the size and shape of objects, movements, color, sound, touch and the user's own body image. During this period, the user's ability to perceive objects through the senses is distorted. He may describe "hearing colors" and "seeing sounds." The ability to make sensible judgments and see common dangers is impaired, making the user susceptible to personal injury. He may also injure others by attempting to drive a car or by operating machinery. After an LSD "trip," the user may suffer acute anxiety or depression for a variable period of time. Flashbacks have been reported days or even months after taking the last dose.

DOM, DOB, MDA, MDMA and 2C-B

Many chemical variations of mescaline and amphetamine have been synthesized for their "feel good" effects. 4-Methyl-2, 5dimethoxyamphetamine (DaM) was introduced into the San Francisco drug scene in the late 1960s, and was nicknamed STP, an acronym for "Serenity, Tranquillity, and Peace." Doses of 1 to 3 milligrams generally produce mood alterations and minor perceptual alterations while larger doses can produce pronounced hallucinations that last from 8 to 10 hours.

Other illicitly manufactured analogues include 4-bromo- 2,5-dimethoxyamphetamine (DaB), 3,4-methylenedioxyamphetamine (MD A), 3,4- methy lenedioxymethamphetamine (MDMA, also referred to as Ecstasy or XTC) and 4-bromo-2,5-dimethoxyphenethylamine (2C-B, NEXUS). These drugs differ from one another in their potency, speed of onset, duration of action and their capacity to modify mood with or without producing overt hallucinations. These drugs are widely used at "raves." (Raves are large all-night dance parties held in unusual settings, such as warehouses or railroad yards, that feature computer-generated, high volume, pulsating music.) The drugs are usually taken orally, sometimes snorted and rarely injected. Because they are produced in clandestine laboratories, they are seldom pure and the amount in a capsule or tablet is likely to vary considerably.

Phencyclidine (PCP) and Related Drugs

In the 1950s, phencyclidine was investigated as an anesthetic but, due to the side effects of confusion and delirium, its development for human use was discontinued. It became commercially available for use as a veterinary anesthetic in the 1960s under the trade name of Semylan and was placed in Schedule III of the CSA. In 1978, due to considerable abuse of phencyclidine, it was transferred to Schedule II of the CSA and manufacturing of Semylan was discontinued. Today, virtually all of the phencyclidine encountered on the illicit market in the U.S. is produced in clandestine laboratories. Phencyclidine, more commonly known as PCP, is illicitly marketed under a number of other names including Angel Dust, Supergrass, Killer Weed, Embalming Fluid, and Rocket Fuel, reflecting the range of its bizarre and volatile effects. In its pure form, it is a white crystalline powder that readily dissolves in water. However, most PCP on the illicit market contains a number of contaminates as a result of makeshift manufacturing causing the color to range from tan to brown and the consistency from powder to a gummy mass. Although sold in tablets and capsules as well as in powder and liquid form, it is commonly applied to a leafy material, such as parsley, mint, oregano or marijuana, and smoked.

The drug's effects are as varied as its appearance. A moderate amount of PCP often causes the user to feel detached, distant and estranged from his surroundings. Numbness, slurred speech and loss of coordination may be accompanied by a sense of strength and invulnerability. A blank stare, rapid and involuntary eye movements, and an exaggerated gait are among the more observable effects. Auditory hallucinations, image distortion, severe mood disorders, and amnesia may also occur. In some users, PCP may cause acute anxiety and a feeling of impending doom, in others paranoia and violent hostility, and in some it may produce a psychoses indistinguishable from schizophrenia. PCP use is associated with a number of risks and many believe it to be one of the most dangerous drugs of abuse.

Modification of the manufacturing process may yield chemically related analogue capable of producing psychic effects similar to PCP. Four of these substances (N-ethyl-l-phenylcyclohexylamine or PCE, l-(phenylcyclohexyl)-pyrrolidine or PCP 1-[1-(2-thienyl)-cyclohexyl]-piperdine or TCP, and 1[l-(2-thienyl) cyclohexyl] pyrrolidine or TCP have been encountered on the illicit market and have been placed in Schedule I of the CSA. LSD is also a Schedule I hallucinogen.

CANNABIS

Cannabis sativa L., the hemp plant, grows wild throughout most of the tropic and temperate regions of the world. Prior to the advent of synthetic fibers, the cannabis plant was cultivated for the tough fiber of its stem. In the United States, cannabis is legitimately grown only for scientific research. In fact, since 1980, the United States has been the only country where cannabis is licitly cultivated for scientific research.

Cannabis contains chemicals called cannabinoids that are unique to the cannabis plant. Among the cannabinoids synthesized by the plant are cannabinol, cannabidiol, cannabinolidic acids, cannabigerol, cannabichromene, and several isomers of tetrahydrocannabinol. One of these, delta-9-tetrahydrocannabinol (THC), is believed to be responsible for most of the characteristic psychoactive effects of cannabis. Research has resulted in development and marketing of dronabinol (Marinol), a product containing synthetic THC, for the control of nausea and vomiting caused by chemotherapeutic agents used in the treatment of cancer, and to stimulate appetite in AIDS patients.

Cannabis products are usually smoked. Their effects are felt within minutes, reach their peak in 10 to 30 minutes, and may linger for two or three hours. The effects experienced often depend upon the experience and expectations of the individual user as well as the activity of the drug itself. Low doses tend to induce a sense of well-being and a dreamy state of relax at on, which may be accompanied by a more vivid sense of sight, smell, taste, and hearing as well as by subtle alterations in thought formation and expression. This state of intoxification may not be noticeable to an observer. However, driving, occupational or household accidents may result from a distortion of time and space relationships and impaired coordination. Stronger doses intensify reactions. The individual may experience shifting sensory imagery, rapidly fluctuating emotions, a flight of fragmentary thoughts with disturbed associations, an altered sense of selfidentity, impaired memory, and a dulling of attention despite an illusion of heightened insight. High doses may result in image distortion, a loss of personal identity, and fantasies and hallucinations.

Three drugs that come from cannabismarijuana, hashish, and hashish oil-are currently distributed on the U.S. illicit market. Having no currently accepted medical use in treatment in the United States, they remain under Schedule I of the CSA. Today, cannabis is carefully illicitly cultivated, both indoors and out, to maximize its THC content, thereby producing the greatest possible psychoactive effect.

Marijuana

Marijuana is the most commonly used illicit drug in America today. The term marijuana, as commonly used, refers to the leaves and flowering tops of the cannabis plant.

A tobacco-like substance produced by drying the leaves and flowering tops of the cannabis plant, marijuana varies significantly in its potency, depending on the source and selection of plant materials used. The form of marijuana known as sinsemilla (Spanish, sin semilla: without seed), derived from the unpollinated female cannabis plant, is preferred for its high THC content.

Marijuana is usually smoked in the form of loosely rolled cigarettes called joints or hollowed out commercial cigars called blunts. Joints and blunts may be laced with a number of adulterants including phencyclidine (PCP), substantially altering the effects and toxicity of these products. Street names for marijuana include pot, grass, weed, Mary Jane, Acupulco Gold, and reefer.

Although marijuana grown in the U.S. was once considered inferior because of a low concentration of THC, advancements in plant selection and cultivation have resulted in highly potent domestic marijuana. In 1974, the average THC content of illicit marijuana was less than one percent; in early 1994, potency averaged 5 percent. The THC of today's sinsemilla ranges up to 17 percent.

Marijuana contains known toxins and cancer-causing chemicals which are stored in fat cells for as long as several months. Marijuana users experience the same health problems as tobacco smokers, such as bronchitis, emphysema and bronchial asthma. Some of the effects of marijuana use also include increased heart rate, dryness of the mouth, reddening of the eyes, impaired motor skills and concentration, and frequently hunger and an increased desire for sweets. Extended use increases risk to the lungs and reproductive system, as well as suppression of the immune system. Occasionally hallucinations, fantasies and paranoia are reported.

Hashish

Hashish consists of the THC-rich resinous material of the cannabis plant, which is collected, dried, and then compressed into a variety of forms, such as balls, cakes, or cookie-like sheets. Pieces are then broken off, placed in pipes and smoked. The Middle East, North Africa, and Pakistan/Afghanistan are the main sources of hashish. The THC content of hashish that reached the United States, where demand is limited, averaged 6 percent in the -1990s.

Hash Oil

The term hash oil is used by illicit drug users and dealers but is a misnomer in suggesting any resemblance to hashish. Hash oil is produced by extracting the cannabinoids from plant material with a solvent. The color and odor of the resulting extract will vary, depending on the type of solvent used. Current samples of hash oil, a viscous liquid ranging from amber to dark brown in color, average about 15 percent The. In terms of its psychoactive effect, a drop or two of this liquid on a cigarette is equal to a single "joint" of marijuana.

STEROIDS

Anabolic steroid abuse has become a national concern. These drugs are used illicitly by weight lifters, body builders, long distance runners, cyclists and others who claim that these drugs give them a competitive advantage and/or improve their physical appearance. Once viewed as a problem associated only with professional athletes, recent reports estimate that 5 percent to 12 percent of male high school students and 1 percent of female students have used anabolic steroids by the time they were seniors. Concerns over a growing illicit market and prevalence of abuse combined with the possibility of harmful long-term effects of steroid use, led Congress in 1991 to place anabolic steroids into Schedule III of the Controlled Substances Act (CSA).

The CSA defines anabolic steroids as any drug or hormonal substance chemically and pharmacologically related to testosterone (other than estrogens, progestins, and corticosteroids), that promotes muscle growth. Most illicit anabolic steroids are sold at gyms, competitions and through mail order operations. For the most part, these substances are smuggled into this country. Those commonly encountered on the illicit market include: boldenone (Equipoise), ethylestrenol (Maxibolin), fluoxymesterone (Halotestin), methandriol, methandrostenolone (Dianabol), methyltestosterone, nandrolone (Durabolin, Deca-Durabolin), oxandrolone (Anavar), oxymetholone (Anadrol), stanozolol (Winstrol), testosterone and trenbolone (Finajet). In addition, a number of bogus or counterfeit products are sold as anabolic steroids.

A limited number of anabolic steroids have been approved for medical and veterinary use. The primary legitimate use of these drugs in humans is for the replacement of inadequate levels of testosterone resulting from a reduction or absence of functioning testes. In veterinary practice, anabolic steroids are used to promote feed efficiency and to improve weight gain, vigor and hair coat. They are also used in veterinary practice to treat anemia and counteract tissue breakdown during illness and trauma.

When used in combination with exercise training and high protein diet, anabolic steroids can promote increased size and strength of muscles, improve endurance and decrease recovery time between workouts. They are taken orally or by intramuscular injection. Users concerned about drug tolerance often take steroids on a schedule called a cycle. A cycle is a period of between 6 and 14 weeks of steroid use followed by a period of abstinence or reduction in use. Additionally, users tend to "stack" the drugs, using multiple drugs concurrently. Although the benefits of these practices are unsubstantiated, most users feel that cycling and stacking enhance the efficiency of the drugs and limit their side effects.

Yet another mode of steroid use is "pyramiding" in which users slowly escalate steroid use (increasing the number of drugs used at one time and/or the dose and frequency of one or more steroids) reaching a peak amount at mid-cycle and gradually tapering the dose toward the end of the cycle. The escalation of steroid use can vary with different types of training. Body builders and weight lifters tend to escalate their dose to a much higher level than do long distance runners or swimmers.

The adverse effects of large doses of multiple anabolic steroids are not well established. However, there is increasing evidence of serious health problems associated with the abuse of these agents, including cardiovascular damage; liver damage and damage to reproductive Physical side effects include elevated blood pressure and cholesterol levels, severe acne, premature balding, reduced sexual function and testicular atrophy. In males, abnormal breast development (gynecomastia) can occur. In females, anabolic steroids have a mas culinizing effect resulting in more body hair, a deeper voice, smaller breasts and fewer menstrual cycles. Several of these effects are irreversible. In adolescents, abuse of these agents may prematurely stop the lengthening of bones resulting in stunted growth.

RELATED TOPICS

CLANDESTINE LABS

Drugs of abuse in the United States come from a variety of sources. Heroin and cocaine, for example, are produced in foreign countries and smuggled into the U.S. Marijuana is cultivated domestically or smuggled from foreign sources. Legitimate pharmaceuticals are diverted to the illicit market. Continuing efforts on the part of state and federal governments to reduce the amount of dangerous and illicit drugs available for abuse, combined with the demand for psychoactive substances, have contributed to the proliferation of clandestine laboratories.

Clandestine laboratories are illicit operations consisting of chemicals and equipment necessary to manufacture controlled substances. The types and numbers of laboratories seized, to a large degree, reflect regional and national trends in the types and amounts of illicit substances that are being manufactured, trafficked and abused. Clandestine laboratories have been found in remote locations like mountain cabins and rural farms. Laboratories are also being operated in single and multifamily residences in urban and suburban neighborhoods where their toxic and explosive fumes can pose a significant threat to the health and safety of local residents.

The production of some substances, such as methamphetamine, PCP, MDMA and methcathinone, requires little sophisticated equipment or knowledge of chemistry; the synthesis of other drugs such as fentanyl and LSD requires much higher levels of expertise and equipment. Some clandestine laboratory operators have little or no training in chemistry and follow underground recipes; others employ chemistry students or professionals as "cooks."

The clandestine production of all drugs is dependent on the availability of essential raw materials. The distribution, sale, import and export of certain chemicals which are important to the manufacture of common illicitly produced substances have been regulated since the enactment of the Chemical Diversion and Trafficking Act of 1988. Enforcement of this and similar state laws has had a significant impact on the availability of chemicals to the clandestine laboratory.

INHALANTS

Inhalants are a chemically diverse group of psychoactive substances composed of organic solvents and volatile substances commonly found in adhesives, lighter fluids, cleaning fluids and paint products. Their easy accessibility, low cost and ease of concealment make inhalants, for many, one of the first substances abused. While not regulated under the CSA, a few states place restrictions on the sale of these products to minors. Studies have indicated that between 5 percent and 15 percent of young people in the United States have tried inhalants, although the vast majority of these youngsters do not become chronic abusers.

Inhalants may be sniffed directly from an open container or "huffed" from a rag soaked in the substance and held to the face. Alternatively, the open container or soaked rag can be placed in a bag where the vapors can concentrate before being inhaled. Although inhalant abusers may prefer one particular substance because of odor or taste, a variety of substances may be used because of their similar effects, availability and cost. Once inhaled, the extensive capillary surface of the lungs allows rapid absorption of the substance and blood levels peak rapidly. Entry into the brain is so fast that the effects of inhalation can resemble the intensity of effects produced by intravenous injection of other psychoactive drugs.

The effects of inhalant intoxication resemble those of alcohol inebriation, with stimulation and loss of inhibition followed by depression at high doses. Users report distortion in perceptions of time and space. Many users experience headache, nausea or vomiting, slurred speech, loss of motor coordination and wheezing. A characteristic "glue sniffer's rash" around the nose and mouth may be seen. An odor of paint or solvents on clothes, skin and breath is sometimes a sign of inhalant abuse.

The chronic use of inhalants has been associated with a number of serious health problems. Glue and paint thinner sniffing in particular produce kidney abnormalities, while the solvents, toluene and trichloroethylene, cause liver toxicity. Memory impairment, attention deficits and diminished non-verbal intelligence have been associated with the abuse of inhalants. Deaths resulting from heart failure, asphyxiation or aspiration have occurred.

Controlled Substances

Drugs	CSA Schedules	Trade or Other Names	Medical Uses
Narcotics			
Heroin	I	Diacetylmorphine, Horse, Smack	None in U.S., Analgesic, Antitussive
Morphine	II	Duramorph, MS-Contin, Roxanol, Oramorph SR	Analgesic
Codeine	II,III,V	Tylenol w/Codeine, Empirin w/Codeine, Robitussin A-C, Fiorinal w/Codeine, APAP w/Codeine	Analgesic, Antitussive
Hydrocodone	II,III	Tussionex, Vicodin, Hycodan, Lorcet	Analgesic, Antitussive
Hydromorphone	II	Dilaudid	Analgesic
Oxycodone	II	Percodan, Percocet, Tylox, Roxicet, Roxicodone	Analgesic
Methadone and LAAM	I,II	Dolophine, Methadose, Levo-alpha-acetylmethadol, Levomethadyl acetate	Analgesic, Treatment of Dependence
Fentanyl and Analogs	I,II	Innovar, Sublimaze, Alfenta, Sufenta, Duragesic	Analgesic, Adjunct to Anesthesia, Anesthetic
Other Narcotics	II,III,IV,V	Percodan, Percocet, Tylox, Opium, Darvon, Talwin [2], Buprenorphine, Meperdine (Pethidine), Demerol	Analgesic, Antidiarrheal
Depressants			
Chloral Hydrate	IV	Noctec, Somnos, Felsules	Hypnotic
Barbiturates	II,III,IV	Amytal, Fiorinal, Nembutal, Seconal, Tuinal, Phenobarbital, Pentobarbital	Anesthetic, anticonvulsant, sedative hypnotic, veterinary euthanasia agent
Benzodiazepines	IV	Ativan, Dalmane, Diazepam, Librium, Xanax, Serax, Valium, Tranxene, Verstran, Versed, Halcion, Paxipam, Restoril	Antianxiety, sedative, anticonvulsant, hypnotic
Glutethimide	II	Doriden	Sedative, hypnotic
Other Depressants	I,II,III,IV	Equanil, Miltown, Noludar, Placidyl, Valmid, Methaqualone	Antianxiety, Sedative, Hypnotic
Stimulants			
Cocaine[1]	II	Coke, Flake, Snow, Crack	Local anesthetic
Amphetamine/Methamphetamine	II	Biphetamine, Desoxyn, Dexedrine, Obetrol, Ice	Attention deficit disorder, narcolepsy, weight control
Methylphenidate	II	Ritalin	Attention deficit disorder, narcolepsy
Other Stimulants	I,II,III,IV	Adipex, Didrex, Ionamin, Melfiat, Plegine, Captagon, Sanorex, Tenuate, Tepanil, Prelu-2, Preludin	Weight control
Cannabis			
Marijuana	I	Pot, Acapulco Gold, Grass, Reefer, Sinsemilla, Thai Sticks	None
Tetrahydrocannabinol	I,II	THC, Marinol	Antinauseant
Hashish and Hashish Oil	I	Hash, Hash oil	None
Hallucinogens			
LSD	I	Acid, Microdot	None
Mescaline and Peyote	I	Mescal, Buttons, Cactus	None
Amphetamine Variants	I	2, 5-DMA, STP, MDA, MDMA, Ecstasy, DOM, DOB	None
Phencyclidine and Analogs	I,II	PCE, PCPy, TCP, PCP, Hog, Loveboat, Angel Dust	None
Other Hallucinogens	I	Bufotenine, Ibogaine, DMT, DET, Psilocybin, Psilocyn	None
Anabolic Steroids			
Testosterone (Cypionate, Enanthate)	III	Depo-Testosterone, Delatestryl	Hypogonadism
Nandrolone (Decanoate, Phenpropionate)	III	Nortestosterone, Durabolin, Deca-Durabolin, Deca	Anemia, breast cancer
Oxymetholone	III	Anadrol-50	Anemia

Uses and Effects

U.S. Department of Justice
Drug Enforcement Administration

Physical Dependence	Psychological Dependence	Tolerance	Duration (Hours)	Usual Method	Possible Effects	Effects of Overdose	Withdrawal Syndome
High	High	Yes	3-6	Injected, sniffed, smoked	● Euphoria	● Slow and shallow breathing	● Watery eyes
High	High	Yes	3-6	Oral, smoked. injected	● Drowsiness	● Clammy skin	● Runny nose
Moderate	Moderate	Yes	3-6	Oral, injected	● Respiratory depression	● Convulsions	● Yawning
High	High	Yes	3-6	Oral		● Coma	● Loss of appetite
High	High	Yes	3-6	Oral, injected	● Constricted pupils	● Possible death	● Irritability
High	High	Yes	4-5	Oral	● Nausea		● Tremors
High	High	Yes	12-72	Oral, injected			● Panic
High	High	Yes	.10-72	Injected, Trans-dermal patch			● Cramps
High-Low	High-Low	Yes	Variable	Oral, injected			● Nausea
							● Chills and sweating
Moderate	Moderate	Yes	5-8	Oral	● Slurred speech	● Shallow respiration	● Anxiety
High-Mod.	High-Mod.	Yes	1-16	Oral, injected	● Disorientation	● Clammy skin	● Insomnia
Low	Low	Yes	4-8	Oral, injected	● Drunken behavior without odor of alcohol	● Dilated pupils	● Tremors
High	Moderate	Yes	4-8	Oral		● Weak and rapid pulse	● Delirium
Moderate	Moderate	Yes	4-8	Oral		● Coma	● Convulsions
						● Possible death	● Possible death
Possible	High	Yes	1-2	Sniffed, smoked. injected	● Increased alertness	● Agitation	● Apathy
Possible	High	Yes	2-4	Oral, injected. smoked	● Excitation	● Increased body temperature	● Long periods of sleep
Possible	High	Yes	2-4	Oral, injected	● Euphoria	● Hallucinations	● Irritability
Possible	High	Yes	2-4	Oral, injected	● Increased pulse rate & blood pressure	● Convulsions	● Depression
					● Insomnia	● Possible death	● Disorientation
					● Loss of appetite		
Unknown	Moderate	Yes	2-4	Smoked, oral	● Euphoria	● Fatigue	● Occasional reports of insomnia
Unknown	Moderate	Yes	2-4	Smoked, oral	● Relaxed inhibitions	● Paranoia	● Hyperactivity
Unknown	Moderate	Yes	2-4	Smoked, oral	● Increased appetite	● Possible psychosis	● Decreased appetite
					● Disorientation		
None	Unknown	Yes	8-12	Oral	● Illusions and hallucinations	● Longer	● Unknown
None	Unknown	Yes	8-12	Oral	● Altered perception of time and distance	● More intensed "trip" episodes	
Unknown	Unknown	Yes	Variable	Oral, injected		● Psychosis	
Unknown	High	Yes	Days	Oral, smoked		● Possible death	
None	Unknown	Possible	Variable	Smoked, oral, injected. sniffed			
Unknown	Unknown	Unknown	14-28 days	Injected	● Virilization	● Unknown	● Possible depression
Unknown	Unknown	Unknown	14-21 days	Injected	● Acne		
Unknown	Unknown	Unknown	24	Oral	● Testicular atrophy		
					● Gynecomastia		
					● Agressive behavior		
					● Edema		

Designated a narcotic under the CSA   ¹ Not designated a narcotic under the CSA

DEPRESSANTS

Schedule II

Trade Name:
Amytal Sodium
Controlled Ingredient:
amobarbital sodium
200 mg

Trade Name:
Doriden
Controlled Ingredient:
glutethimide
500 mg

Trade Name:
Nembutal Sodium
Controlled Ingredient:
pentobarbital sodium
100 mg

Trade Name:
Seconal Sodium
Controlled Ingredient:
secobarbital sodium
100 mg

Trade Name:
Tuinal
Controlled Ingredients:
amobarbital sodium 100 mg
secobarbital sodium 100 mg

Schedule IV

Trade Name:
Ativan
Controlled Ingredient:
lorazepam
0.5 mg

Trade Name:
Ativan
Controlled Ingredient:
lorazepam
1 mg

Trade Name:
Ativan
Controlled Ingredient:
lorazepam
2 mg

Trade Name:
Centrax
Controlled Ingredient:
prazepam
5 mg

Trade Name:
Centrax
Controlled Ingredient:
prazepam 10 mg

Trade Name:
Centrax
Controlled Ingredient:
prazepam 10 mg

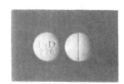

Trade Name:
Chloral Hydrate
Controlled Ingredient:
chloral hydrate
500 mg

Trade Name:
Dalmane
Controlled Ingredient:
flurazepam hydrochloride
15 mg

Trade Name:
Dalmane
Controlled Ingredient:
flurazepam hydrochloride
30 mg

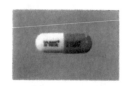

Trade Name:
Equanil
Controlled Ingredient:
meprobamate
200 mg

Trade Name:
Equanil
Controlled Ingredient:
meprobamate
400 mg

Trade Name:
Halcion
Controlled Ingredient:
triazolam
0.25 mg

Trade Name:
Halcion
Controlled Ingredient:
triazolam
0.5 mg

Trade Name:
Restoril
Controlled Ingredient:
temazepam
15 mg

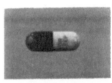

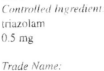

Trade Name:
Librium
Controlled Ingredient:
chlordiazepoxide hydrochloride
5 mg

Trade Name:
Restoril
Controlled Ingredient:
temazepam
30 mg

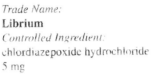

Trade Name:
Librium
Controlled Ingredient:
chlordiazepoxide hydrochloride
10 mg

Trade Name:
Serax
Controlled Ingredient:
oxazepam
10 mg

Trade Name:
Librium
Controlled Ingredient:
chlordiazepoxide hydrochloride
25 mg

Trade Name:
Serax
Controlled Ingredient:
oxazepam
15 mg

Trade Name:
Miltown 400
Controlled Ingredient:
meprobamate
400 mg

Trade Name:
Serax
Controlled Ingredient:
oxazepam 15 mg

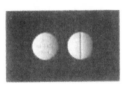

Trade Name:
Miltown 600
Controlled Ingredient:
meprobamate
600 mg

Trade Name:
Serax
Controlled Ingredient:
oxazepam
30 mg

Trade Name:
Placidyl
Controlled Ingredient:
ethchlorvynol
200 mg

Trade Name:
Tranxene
Controlled Ingredient:
clorazepate dipotassium
3.75 mg

Trade Name:
Placidyl
Controlled Ingredient:
ethchlorvynol
500 mg

Trade Name:
Tranxene
Controlled Ingredient:
clorazepate dipotassium
7.5 mg

Trade Name:
Placidyl
Controlled Ingredient:
ethchlorvynol
750 mg

Trade Name:
Tranxene
Controlled Ingredient:
clorazepate dipotassium
15 mg

Trade Name:
Valium
Controlled Ingredient:
diazepam
2 mg

Trade Name:
Valium
Controlled Ingredient:
diazepam
5 mg

Trade Name:
Valium
Controlled Ingredient:
diazepam
10 mg

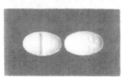

Trade Name:
Xanax
Controlled Ingredient:
alprazolam
0.25 mg

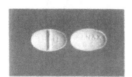

Trade Name:
Xanax
Controlled Ingredient:
alprazolam
0.5 mg

Trade Name:
Xanax
Controlled Ingredient:
alprazolam
1 mg

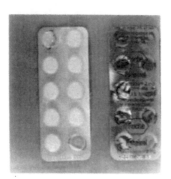

Rohyphnol contains the controlled ingredient flunitrazepam hydrochloride. Pictured here is a 2-mg tablet with packaging. "Roofies," as they are known on the street, are sold inexpensively in Mexico. They are smuggled into the United States where they have recently become a problem among American teens. The problem is rapidly spreading from the American southwest to other parts of the United States.

ANSWER SHEET

TEST NO. _____ PART _____ TITLE OF POSITION _____

(AS GIVEN IN EXAMINATION ANNOUNCEMENT · INCLUDE OPTION, IF ANY)

PLACE OF EXAMINATION _____ DATE_____

(CITY OR TOWN)   (STATE)

RATING

USE THE SPECIAL PENCIL. MAKE GLOSSY BLACK MARKS.

	A B C D E		A B C D E		A B C D E		A B C D E		A B C D E
1	‖ ‖ ‖ ‖ ‖	26	‖ ‖ ‖ ‖ ‖	51	‖ ‖ ‖ ‖ ‖	76	‖ ‖ ‖ ‖ ‖	101	‖ ‖ ‖ ‖ ‖
2	‖ ‖ ‖ ‖ ‖	27	‖ ‖ ‖ ‖ ‖	52	‖ ‖ ‖ ‖ ‖	77	‖ ‖ ‖ ‖ ‖	102	‖ ‖ ‖ ‖ ‖
3	‖ ‖ ‖ ‖ ‖	28	‖ ‖ ‖ ‖ ‖	53	‖ ‖ ‖ ‖ ‖	78	‖ ‖ ‖ ‖ ‖	103	‖ ‖ ‖ ‖ ‖
4	‖ ‖ ‖ ‖ ‖	29	‖ ‖ ‖ ‖ ‖	54	‖ ‖ ‖ ‖ ‖	79	‖ ‖ ‖ ‖ ‖	104	‖ ‖ ‖ ‖ ‖
5	‖ ‖ ‖ ‖ ‖	30	‖ ‖ ‖ ‖ ‖	55	‖ ‖ ‖ ‖ ‖	80	‖ ‖ ‖ ‖ ‖	105	‖ ‖ ‖ ‖ ‖
6	‖ ‖ ‖ ‖ ‖	31	‖ ‖ ‖ ‖ ‖	56	‖ ‖ ‖ ‖ ‖	81	‖ ‖ ‖ ‖ ‖	106	‖ ‖ ‖ ‖ ‖
7	‖ ‖ ‖ ‖ ‖	32	‖ ‖ ‖ ‖ ‖	57	‖ ‖ ‖ ‖ ‖	82	‖ ‖ ‖ ‖ ‖	107	‖ ‖ ‖ ‖ ‖
8	‖ ‖ ‖ ‖ ‖	33	‖ ‖ ‖ ‖ ‖	58	‖ ‖ ‖ ‖ ‖	83	‖ ‖ ‖ ‖ ‖	108	‖ ‖ ‖ ‖ ‖
9	‖ ‖ ‖ ‖ ‖	34	‖ ‖ ‖ ‖ ‖	59	‖ ‖ ‖ ‖ ‖	84	‖ ‖ ‖ ‖ ‖	109	‖ ‖ ‖ ‖ ‖
10	‖ ‖ ‖ ‖ ‖	35	‖ ‖ ‖ ‖ ‖	60	‖ ‖ ‖ ‖ ‖	85	‖ ‖ ‖ ‖ ‖	110	‖ ‖ ‖ ‖ ‖

Make only ONE mark for each answer. Additional and stray marks may be
counted as mistakes. In making corrections, erase errors COMPLETELY.

	A B C D E		A B C D E		A B C D E		A B C D E		A B C D E
11	‖ ‖ ‖ ‖ ‖	36	‖ ‖ ‖ ‖ ‖	61	‖ ‖ ‖ ‖ ‖	86	‖ ‖ ‖ ‖ ‖	111	‖ ‖ ‖ ‖ ‖
12	‖ ‖ ‖ ‖ ‖	37	‖ ‖ ‖ ‖ ‖	62	‖ ‖ ‖ ‖ ‖	87	‖ ‖ ‖ ‖ ‖	112	‖ ‖ ‖ ‖ ‖
13	‖ ‖ ‖ ‖ ‖	38	‖ ‖ ‖ ‖ ‖	63	‖ ‖ ‖ ‖ ‖	88	‖ ‖ ‖ ‖ ‖	113	‖ ‖ ‖ ‖ ‖
14	‖ ‖ ‖ ‖ ‖	39	‖ ‖ ‖ ‖ ‖	64	‖ ‖ ‖ ‖ ‖	89	‖ ‖ ‖ ‖ ‖	114	‖ ‖ ‖ ‖ ‖
15	‖ ‖ ‖ ‖ ‖	40	‖ ‖ ‖ ‖ ‖	65	‖ ‖ ‖ ‖ ‖	90	‖ ‖ ‖ ‖ ‖	115	‖ ‖ ‖ ‖ ‖
16	‖ ‖ ‖ ‖ ‖	41	‖ ‖ ‖ ‖ ‖	66	‖ ‖ ‖ ‖ ‖	91	‖ ‖ ‖ ‖ ‖	116	‖ ‖ ‖ ‖ ‖
17	‖ ‖ ‖ ‖ ‖	42	‖ ‖ ‖ ‖ ‖	67	‖ ‖ ‖ ‖ ‖	92	‖ ‖ ‖ ‖ ‖	117	‖ ‖ ‖ ‖ ‖
18	‖ ‖ ‖ ‖ ‖	43	‖ ‖ ‖ ‖ ‖	68	‖ ‖ ‖ ‖ ‖	93	‖ ‖ ‖ ‖ ‖	118	‖ ‖ ‖ ‖ ‖
19	‖ ‖ ‖ ‖ ‖	44	‖ ‖ ‖ ‖ ‖	69	‖ ‖ ‖ ‖ ‖	94	‖ ‖ ‖ ‖ ‖	119	‖ ‖ ‖ ‖ ‖
20	‖ ‖ ‖ ‖ ‖	45	‖ ‖ ‖ ‖ ‖	70	‖ ‖ ‖ ‖ ‖	95	‖ ‖ ‖ ‖ ‖	120	‖ ‖ ‖ ‖ ‖
21	‖ ‖ ‖ ‖ ‖	46	‖ ‖ ‖ ‖ ‖	71	‖ ‖ ‖ ‖ ‖	96	‖ ‖ ‖ ‖ ‖	121	‖ ‖ ‖ ‖ ‖
22	‖ ‖ ‖ ‖ ‖	47	‖ ‖ ‖ ‖ ‖	72	‖ ‖ ‖ ‖ ‖	97	‖ ‖ ‖ ‖ ‖	122	‖ ‖ ‖ ‖ ‖
23	‖ ‖ ‖ ‖ ‖	48	‖ ‖ ‖ ‖ ‖	73	‖ ‖ ‖ ‖ ‖	98	‖ ‖ ‖ ‖ ‖	123	‖ ‖ ‖ ‖ ‖
24	‖ ‖ ‖ ‖ ‖	49	‖ ‖ ‖ ‖ ‖	74	‖ ‖ ‖ ‖ ‖	99	‖ ‖ ‖ ‖ ‖	124	‖ ‖ ‖ ‖ ‖
25	‖ ‖ ‖ ‖ ‖	50	‖ ‖ ‖ ‖ ‖	75	‖ ‖ ‖ ‖ ‖	100	‖ ‖ ‖ ‖ ‖	125	‖ ‖ ‖ ‖ ‖

ANSWER SHEET

TEST NO. ________ PART ______ TITLE OF POSITION ________________________
(AS GIVEN IN EXAMINATION ANNOUNCEMENT - INCLUDE OPTION, IF ANY)

PLACE OF EXAMINATION ________________________ DATE ________
(CITY OR TOWN) (STATE)

RATING

USE THE SPECIAL PENCIL. MAKE GLOSSY BLACK MARKS.

	A	B	C	D	E		A	B	C	D	E		A	B	C	D	E		A	B	C	D	E		A	B	C	D	E
1						26						51						76						101					
2						27						52						77						102					
3						28						53						78						103					
4						29						54						79						104					
5						30						55						80						105					
6						31						56						81						106					
7						32						57						82						107					
8						33						58						83						108					
9						34						59						84						109					
10						35						60						85						110					

Make only ONE mark for each answer. Additional and stray marks may be counted as mistakes. In making corrections, erase errors COMPLETELY.

	A	B	C	D	E		A	B	C	D	E		A	B	C	D	E		A	B	C	D	E		A	B	C	D	E
11						36						61						86						111					
12						37						62						87						112					
13						38						63						88						113					
14						39						64						89						114					
15						40						65						90						115					
16						41						66						91						116					
17						42						67						92						117					
18						43						68						93						118					
19						44						69						94						119					
20						45						70						95						120					
21						46						71						96						121					
22						47						72						97						122					
23						48						73						98						123					
24						49						74						99						124					
25						50						75						100						125					